Geoffrey Dean

The Orphic I
A Philosophical Approach to Musical Collaboration

STUDIES IN HISTORICAL PHILOSOPHY

Editor: Alexander Gungov

Consulting Editor: Donald Phillip Verene

ISSN 2629-0316

1 Dustin Peone
  Memory as Philosophy
  The Theory and Practice of
  Philosophical Recollection
  ISBN 978-3-8382-1336-1

2 Raymond Barfield
  The Poetic Apriori:
  Philosophical Imagination
  in a Meaningful Universe
  ISBN 978-3-8382-1350-7

3 Jennifer Lobo Meeks
  Allegory in Early Greek
  Philosophy
  ISBN 978-3-8382-1425-2

4 Vanessa Freerks
  Baudrillard with Nietzsche
  and Heidegger: Towards a
  Genealogical Analysis
  ISBN 978-3-8382-1474-0

5 Thora Ilin Bayer and
  Donald Phillip Verene
  Philosophical Ideas
  A Historical Study
  ISBN 978-3-8382-1585-3

6 Jeffrey Andrew Barash
  Shadows of Being
  Encounters with Heidegger in
  Political Theory and Historical
  Reflection
  ISBN 978-3-8382-1485-6

7 Donald Phillip Verene
  The Philosophic Spirit
  Its Meaning and Presence
  ISBN 978-3-8382-1781-9

8 Geoffrey Dean
  The Orphic I
  A Philosophical Approach to
  Musical Collaboration
  ISBN 978-3-8382-1629-4

Geoffrey Dean

THE ORPHIC I
A Philosophical Approach to Musical Collaboration

Bibliografische Information der Deutschen Nationalbibliothek
Die Deutsche Nationalbibliothek verzeichnet diese Publikation in der Deutschen Nationalbibliografie; detaillierte bibliografische Daten sind im Internet über http://dnb.d-nb.de abrufbar.

Bibliographic information published by the Deutsche Nationalbibliothek
Die Deutsche Nationalbibliothek lists this publication in the Deutsche Nationalbibliografie; detailed bibliographic data are available in the Internet at http://dnb.d-nb.de.

ISBN-13: 978-3-8382-1629-4
© *ibidem*-Verlag, Stuttgart 2023
Alle Rechte vorbehalten

Das Werk einschließlich aller seiner Teile ist urheberrechtlich geschützt. Jede Verwertung außerhalb der engen Grenzen des Urheberrechtsgesetzes ist ohne Zustimmung des Verlages unzulässig und strafbar. Dies gilt insbesondere für Vervielfältigungen, Übersetzungen, Mikroverfilmungen und elektronische Speicherformen sowie die Einspeicherung und Verarbeitung in elektronischen Systemen.

All rights reserved. No part of this publication may be reproduced, stored in or introduced into a retrieval system, or transmitted, in any form, or by any means (electronic, mechanical, photocopying, recording or otherwise) without the prior written permission of the publisher. Any person who does any unauthorized act in relation to this publication may be liable to criminal prosecution and civil claims for damages.

Printed in the EU

Contents

Preface 7

Part I: An Aesthetics of Social Awareness and Participation

Chapter 1
Heidegger and Hegel: Art as the Happening of Truth 13
    On the History of Philosophy 15
    Aletheia and the Nature of Truth 17
    The Work of Art as Illuminating Projection 23
    Reclaiming the Happening of Truth 33

Chapter 2
Dewey and Gadamer: Art as Community of Experience 39
    Two Anti-Foundational Approaches to Aesthetics 40
    The Post-Philosophical Debate 42
    Reunifying Art and Experience 44
    The Work of Art as Expressive Object and as Symbol 51

Part II: Orphic Intersubjectivity

Chapter 3
The Performer as Co-Composer:
"Hearing As" and the Creative Orphic "I" 59
    Orpheus, Inspired Poet-Musician of Antiquity 61
    Ricoeurian Implications of the Orpheus Myth 65
    Lazar Nikolov, A Modern-Day Orpheus 69
    Creative Orphic Intersubjectivity 73

Chapter 4
Consensual Empathic Manipulation: Listener–Performer Identification and the Interpretative Orphic "I" 77

    Philosophical and Psychological Theories of Empathy 79

    Perceived Authenticity in Music 86

    Interpretative Orphic Intersubjectivity 90

Part III: Ensemble Ethics

Chapter 5
Cultural Values in Music:
Control and Conversation in String Quartet Playing 97

    Play, Festival, and Musicking 98

    Communitarian Conceptions of Musical Utopia 102

    Core Values in String Quartet Performance Traditions 106

    Quartet Playing Styles of the Dimov and Sofia Quartets 114

Chapter 6
The Ethics of Entrainment: Music-Making and Habermasian Practical Discourse 119

    Habermas' Unity of Reason and Discourse Ethics 120

    The Care-Free Empathy of Mutual Perspective-taking 123

    The Music-Making Situation as an Ethical Model 127

    Prosocial Interaction in Music Improvisation Projects 133

Bibliography 139
Index 151

Preface

Presaged by the aesthetics of Heidegger, Dewey, and Gadamer, a mainstream philosophical approach to music of recent decades refutes the primacy of the musical work as an object and recasts music as a type of human experience. Reflecting the intersubjective refocusing of philosophical inquiry in the twentieth century, this approach centers on music as "something lived through...a musical field [that] holds participants together," and suggests that the work in and of itself has no meaning, existing only to give musicians something to perform.[1] My main focus in this study is on the interactions of the participants as they engage in the social practices of music creation, performance, and listening.

Recalling Heidegger's restoration of the Greek *aletheia* (truth as unconcealedness) over truth as certainty and drawing on the commonality of pragmatic and hermeneutic principles, I pursue an intersubjective approach to understanding music as a collaborative activity. By incorporating insights gained from my own professional experiences as a performing musician, I have chosen to embrace my own position within music-making traditions. Because these experiences have taken place within a unique intercultural context—that of an American musician working in Bulgaria—my perspective is perhaps as unique as it is potentially flawed or limited. Through an examination of different aspects of my musical activities in Bulgaria, I attempt to bridge the gap between abstract philosophical theory and actual musical practice.

My collaboration with the distinguished Bulgarian composer Lazar Nikolov on his solo composition, *From the Music of Orpheus*, suggested to me a reinterpretation of the Orpheus myth. By transposing the Heideggerian "seeing as"—as applied by Paul Ricoeur in his theory of semantic innovation—to "hearing as," I apply Ricoeur's hermeneutic interpretation of Husserl's concept of imaginative transfer to the composer's collaborative relationship with those who perform his or her music. Through what I call *creative Orphic intersubjectivity*, the composer finds creative inspiration by identifying with a real or imagined performer as a kind of completion of the composer's Orphic self. A central component of Nikolov's creative process, this identification allows the composer to

---

[1] Philip Alperson, "Introduction: The Philosophy of Music," in *What is Music? An Introduction to the Philosophy of Music*, ed. P. Alperson (University Park, PA: The Pennsylvania State University Press, 1987), 14.

achieve self-consciousness as the product of consciousness of another, as Orpheus is transformed by being revealed to himself when he looks back at Eurydice.

The performative collaborative approaches I experienced while working with composers Dimiter Christoff and Petros Ovsepyan led me to look at imaginative transfer and the associated concept of empathy in a different light—through the prism of the multimodality of musical performance. With the support of Dewey's statement on manipulation as art in incipiency, I suggest that audience members willingly perceive the performer's dishonest signals as sincere through what I term *consensual empathic manipulation*. Related to it is *interpretative Orphic intersubjectivity*, whereby a performative composer identifies with a performer later in the creative process, while they work together to shape a musical interpretation that is both aurally and visually compelling for the seeing listener.

My years of international concert activity as the cellist of two leading Bulgarian string quartets led me to explore the cultural values embedded in the social interactions of those who perform music together. Examining communitarian aspects of Gadamer's aesthetics and MacIntyre's ideas on tradition, I suggest that the participatory act of music-making is both a model for and exemplar of specific intercultural relationships. A division along liberal and communitarian lines can be observed in the distinction between what I call the *conversation and control models of string quartet playing*. My own intercultural chamber music experiences have shown that the core values of individual ensemble members cannot be upheld unless they are grounded in what I refer to as a set of unifying communitarian ideals that govern the ensemble's collective work.

My performance projects involving informal and improvised group music-making among people from divergent cultural backgrounds, and having little or no previous musical interaction, support my conception of *entrainment ethics*. I propose that music performance situations based on entrainment—the innate perception of repeating patterns within a time frame—provide a universally valid ground for practices undertaken to obtain group consensus. Interactive music-making can therefore precede and model the public discourse at the heart of Habermas' Discourse Ethics.

Habermasian thought brings together several interconnected strands of my inquiry into the nature of musical collaboration. Habermas has been outspoken about his decisive turn toward intersubjectivity as a response to what he sees as the exhaustion of the philosophy of the subject. He stands out among the present-day philosophers who draw on a broad variety of scholarly sources, uniting the continental and analytical traditions. His intentionally de-limited conception of empathy as the social cognition of mutual perspective-taking offers a firm philosophical foundation for a fruitful final variation on the workings of empathy in music.

I gratefully acknowledge Prof. Alexander Gungov of Sofia University, without whose expert guidance and constant encouragement I never would have considered writing a study of this nature, let alone carried the project through to completion; Prof. Dimiter Christoff, who magnanimously entrusted to me the (co-)interpretation of his cello music and inspired so many of my earlier writings on music; Prof. Lazar Nikolov, who provided my earliest exposures to contemporary Bulgarian music and my earliest opportunities to perform it; Prof. Artin Potourlian, Roumen Balyozov, and Mihail Goleminov, and the many other Bulgarian composers with whom I have had the honor of collaborating over the years; Mario Angelov, Georgita Boyadzhieva, Rossen Idealov, Ganka Nedelcheva, Biliana Vutchkova, Helen Bledsoe and the inimitable Anssi Karttunen, who showed me what long-term dedication to new music, and authentic artistry in its performance, could look like; my colleagues in the Dimov and Sofia Quartets, the Stankov-Radionov Duo, and at the Ardenza Foundation of Sofia, especially Daniela Dikova and Galina Koycheva, for a sustained immersion in chamber music performance that took us on so many far-flung musical adventures; Ekaterina Docheva, Elena Dragostinova, Natalia Ilieva, and Anda Palieva, for their unflagging support for my festival of American and Bulgarian music, and Julia M. Watkins, whose encouragement while president of the American University in Bulgaria helped get the festival off the ground in the first place; Perry Townsend and Petros Ovsepyan, two of my earliest composer-collaborators, who introduced me to new, unsuspected worlds of sound; Sophia Högstadius, Laura Geier, and Myriam De Bonte, who opened my eyes to the diverse multicultural intersections of music and community through our ethno-music collaborations; Dragomir Yossifov and Goritsa Naidenova, for setting a consistently high bar for encyclopedic erudition; everyone else in my musical family in Europe and the U. S.; my wife Christa and daughter Vera, for giving me daily strength and confidence through their unbounded love, matched by their equally unbounded patience; and my parents, for everything, from the start.

Part I

An Aesthetics of Social Awareness and Participation

Chapter 1

Heidegger and Hegel: Art as the Happening of Truth

During the 1930s, Martin Heidegger (1889–1976) was one of several eminent philosophers giving significant attention to questions of aesthetics. John Dewey gave a series of lectures at Harvard University that was soon published as *Art as Experience*.[1] Ludwig Wittgenstein lectured on art at Cambridge University from 1930 to 1933, and again in 1938.[2] The second version of Walter Benjamin's essay "The Work of Art in the Age of its Technical Reproducibility" appeared in 1936.[3] Heidegger's most extended treatments of art, *The Will to Power as Art* (the first of several series of his lectures on Nietzsche)[4] and "The Origin of the Work of Art" (originally given as a lecture in Freiburg, Zurich, and Frankfurt, and later published as an essay), date from this same decade.[5]

In this chapter I will examine important ideas of "The Origin of the Work of Art" in relation to Heidegger's magnum opus, *Being and Time*,[6] and in terms of a discourse with Hegelian thought suggested to me by Hegel's *Lectures on the History of Philosophy*[7] and Heidegger's discussion

---

1 John Dewey, *Art as Experience* (New York: Perigee, 1934).
2 Ludwig Wittgenstein, *Lectures and Conversations on Aesthetics, Psychology, and Religious Belief*, ed. C. Barrett (Oxford: Blackwell, 1966); George Moore, "Wittgenstein's Lectures, 1930–1933" in *Aesthetics*, ed. H. Osborne (London: Oxford University Press, 1972), 86–88.
3 Walter Benjamin, "The Work of Art in the Age of Its Technological Reproducibility: Second Version," in *The Work of Art in the Age of Its Technological Reproducibility and Other Writings on Media* (Cambridge, MA: Belnap Press, 2008).
4 Martin Heidegger, *Nietzsche I: The Will to Power as Art*, trans. D. Krell (New York: Harper and Row, 1979).
5 Martin Heidegger, "The Origin of the Work of Art," in *Poetry, Language, Thought*, trans. A. Hofstadter (New York: Harper and Row, 1971), 73. Referred to hereafter as *OWA*.
6 Martin Heidegger, *Being and Time*, trans. J. Macquarrie and E. Robinson (Oxford: Blackwell, 1962). Originally published in 1927, *Being and Time* is referred to hereafter as *BT*.
7 Georg Wilhelm Friedrich Hegel, *Hegel's Lectures on the History of Philosophy*, trans. E. S. Haldane and F. H. Simpson (London: Routledge and Kegan Paul, 1892). Referred to hereafter as *LHP*.

of the history of philosophy in "Hegel and the Greeks."[8] In the epilogue of *OWA*, Heidegger directly addresses Hegel's pronouncements concerning the end of art. The epilogue is structurally and thematically reminiscent of Heidegger's treatment of Hegel's conception of time at the end of *Being and Time*.

Heidegger's aesthetic ideas are directly linked to his conception of truth as *aletheia*—truth as unconcealedness (a becoming apparent) rather than Hegelian truth as certainty—and to his understanding of Dasein as primordially both irreducibly situated and intersubjective—"Being-in-the-world" and "Being-with-others." Dasein has a pre-given understanding of being that functions like Husserl's lifeworld to ground its existence within a world. For Heidegger this world is a practical totality in which we participate actively, involving ourselves in relationships with tools that are "ready-to-hand," not just theoretically "present-at-hand." Instead of approaching the work of art as an isolated object, Heidegger rejects the aestheticizing of thought that has resulted in what Gadamer later called the "alienation of aesthetic consciousness"[9] and interrogates the work of art as to its Being. Discussing the work of art in terms of illuminating projection, Heidegger resituates it in the world, demonstrating how the work "works" as a happening of truth that suggests new possibilities of Being to those who devote themselves to understanding it.

The deep social awareness exhibited by specific musical works of the American twentieth century seems to redress Heidegger's concern that art is no longer a happening of truth. For me, these works *are* happenings of truth. They demonstrate how several generations of American composers have focused their art on questions related to our intersubjective "Being-in-the-world," illuminating potential new worlds by gathering participants, documenting events, or prophesizing future needs or outcomes.

---

8   Martin Heidegger, "Hegel and the Greeks," trans. R. Metcalf, in *Pathmarks* (Cambridge: Cambridge University Press, 1998), 323–36. A lecture given at the Conference of the Academy of Sciences, Heidelberg, July 26, 1958.

9   Hans-Georg Gadamer, "The Universality of the Hermeneutical Problem," in *The Continental Philosophy Reader*, ed. R. Kearney and M. Rainwater (New York: Routledge, 1995), 112. Gadamer suggests that alienation of aesthetic consciousness occurs when we focus on an object of aesthetic judgment without receiving that object "in terms of what it says" and "its place in the world where men live together." It involves a closing off of the self that prevents us from being receptive "to the immediate claim of that which grasps us," and it is inherited from Kantian "disinterested contemplation."

On the History of Philosophy

In *BT*, Heidegger interrogates Dasein as to its Being. In *OWA* he approaches the work of art in a similar way. In both cases Heidegger's method is both indebted to and a significant departure from that of Hegel. In *OWA* Heidegger's argumentation seems to approach Hegel's conception of dialectical progress through ascending historical stages. Although Heidegger never explicitly endorses Hegelian dialectic or cumulative history, in *OWA* he does identify specific historical stages, both in the history of art[10] and in the everyday, ordinary understanding of the concept of "thingness."[11]

For Hegel, each stage in the history of philosophy incorporates new thought by in part refuting and in part building on the previous stages of thought, in an ascending movement toward universal Truth. While not rejecting the truth of earlier philosophy—he conceives of truth as outside of time—Hegel assumes that later stages in the history of philosophy are a priori closer to Truth and prioritizes the German thought of his own time as closest to absolute Truth. Accordingly, the Aristotelian concept of "unity of Being" is delimited in Hegel's system:[12] while insisting that no philosophical thought is ever "past,"[13] Hegel views earlier philosophies primarily in accord with an earlier time and historical context and cautions against interpretations of earlier philosophies that attribute to their originators intellectual constructs that were in fact developed in later stages.

Heidegger announces near the outset of *OWA* that "when we think the Being of beings...it is necessary beforehand that the barriers of our preconceptions fall away and that the current pseudo concepts be set aside."[14] This is a restatement of his phenomenological approach in *BT* to destroying history as a prerequisite for his ontological investigation of Dasein's being. By destroying history, by peeling back the layers of thought—the accumulated "ordinary" interpretations—Heidegger sets the stage for a new Interpretation that does not rely on constructs so deeply ingrained in average everyday thinking that their influence on our thinking is not even noticed, but obstructs our ability to understand the primordial presuppositions that ground our existence. In this way the destruction of phenomenological method is also construction, as Heidegger explains

---

10   Heidegger, *OWA*, 74.
11   Ibid., 20–38.
12   Hegel, *LHP*, 49.
13   Ibid., 8–19.
14   Heidegger, *OWA*, 38.

elsewhere.[15] By going back to the origins, Heidegger accords a place of honor not to later German thought, but to ancient Greek philosophy. From the beginning of *BT* Heidegger is explicit that he is not merely reinterpreting Aristotle. He believes that the concept of unity of Being had not been thoroughly investigated before his own account, and while indebted to Aristotle, Heidegger's retrograde quest for a primordial (pre-philosophical) ground descends past Aristotle as well.

The progress of Heidegger's investigation of Dasein's being in *BT* is itself a demonstration of the ecstatico-horizonal unity of temporality that Heidegger explains in Part III of Division Two.[16] His arguments move forward by moving backward, each step seemingly widening the gap between how inauthentic Dasein *thinks* and how authentic Dasein *is*, but always revealing that both inauthentic and authentic ways of being are bound up together in the circular embrace that forms Dasein's Being-in-the-World. As he descends toward ever greater primordiality in his exposure of the existential totality of Dasein, Heidegger is also engaged in a kind of forward progress à la Hegel. A rebuilding of history is taking place. At every juncture Heidegger insists on examining the traditional understandings of concepts, not with a view to discard them, but rather to find their essential place in our way of Being. This progress is more of a leveling-off than an ascent because these later traditional understandings conceal the primordial ones.

Heidegger's decision to specifically discuss Hegel's conception of time in the final sections of *BT*, while showing his indebtedness to Hegelian thought, also seems to signal that his conception of temporality as the meaning of Dasein moves beyond that thought. In Heidegger's account of Hegel's conception of time, time is defined as "an irreversible succession" and history is understood "as happening *within-time*."[17] Heidegger's own primordial conception of temporality makes time accessible in the reverse direction as well, as the multi-directionality of the structure of *BT* illustrates.

As Heidegger periodically reiterates in both *BT* and *OWA*, a seemingly circular logic is necessary. Without naming it, he defends what is commonly known as the "hermeneutic circle," where the expected results of the inquiry are presupposed at the outset. This circularity corresponds

---

15   Martin Heidegger, *The Basic Problems of Phenomenology*, trans. A. Hofstadter (Bloomington: Indiana University Press, 1975), 37–42.
16   Heidegger, *BT*, 349–80.
17   Ibid., 478–9.

to the unity of motions in the overall trajectory of *BT* and the overarching "*is*" of Dasein; this unity seems to confirm Heidegger's conception of authentic temporality as finite. In *LHP*, Hegel posits a similarly circular process of development as it relates to thought, stating that synthesis "must be represented not as a straight line drawn out into vague infinity, but as a circle returning within itself."[18] There is also a circularity in Dasein's essential way of Being, for example in the way that Dasein, heeding the call of conscience, returns to itself from its lostness in the they.[19]

Heidegger's progress in *OWA* also takes him back to the origins and forward to Hegel, whose judgment that art is somehow past[20] Heidegger considers in the epilogue of the essay. In the earlier "Thing and Work" section of *OWA*, Heidegger's account of the three "self-evident" interpretations of "the thingness of the thing...predominant in the course of Western thought" and "now in everyday use"[21] suggests a progress from the time of the ancient Greeks that is also a leveling off rather than an ascent. When he speaks of the appropriation of Greek words into Roman thought, Heidegger finds that "*trans*lation" has taken place as Latin words representing "a different way of thinking" have concealed the "basic Greek experience of the Being of beings in the sense of presence." The transfer to Latin symbolizes the separation of a thing's properties from its pre-existing core or ground—from its Being. In his discussion of the work of art in *OWA*, Heidegger reunites properties and ground, revealing how the work exists and functions in the world, and thereby rescuing it from the "rootlessness of Western thought."[22] As in *BT*, this is a progress that descends, moving backwards toward uncovering the primordial essence of the work of art. Heidegger makes these downward steps explicit in statements such as the following: "We must try to understand **even more essentially** what...could be defined as the work-being of the work."[23]

Aletheia and the Nature of Truth

Heidegger's progress is made possible by the resoluteness of Dasein's essential disclosedness, its "being-uncovered," a concept Heidegger illuminates by interpreting the Greek word *aletheia* as a pre-philosophical

---

18 Hegel, *LHP*, 27.
19 Heidegger, *BT*, 270–1.
20 In *Lectures on Aesthetics (Vorlesungen uber die Asthetik)*.
21 Heidegger, *OWA*, 22.
22 Ibid., 23; Heidegger's emphasis.
23 Ibid., 59; my emphasis.

understanding of truth as unconcealedness. Heidegger discusses aletheia specifically in both the final section of *BT* Division One and in *OWA*. In *OWA* and more directly in "Hegel and the Greeks," Heidegger challenges the "scientific" conception of truth as certainty or correctness that Hegel inherits from modern philosophical method and continues to endorse. Heidegger finds the origin of the work of art in the unity of beauty and truth expressed by aletheia; this origin has been hidden by the subsequent "change of the nature of truth."[24] Heidegger's concern with the relationship of aletheia to art dates to least as early as 1924, when his reading of Aristotle's *Nicomachean Ethics* led him to conclude that "art is a dianoietic virtue or excellence of which human Dasein is capable, and it owes that excellence to its disclosing character. Art is an active mode of *aletheuein*, of disclosing beings; it is a capacity to put *aletheia* into work."[25]

As he did in the final pages of *BT*, Heidegger directly addresses Hegel in the epilogue of *OWA*. Quoting Hegel's declaration in *Lectures on Aesthetics* that art is "something past," Heidegger insists that, despite "the rise of many new art works and movements" since Hegel's last lectures on aesthetics a century earlier, Hegel's judgment "remains in force." Heidegger rephrases Hegel's judgment as a question that must be confronted: "is art still an essential and necessary way in which that truth happens which is decisive for our historical existence…?"[26]

Hegel sees art as "something past" in the sense that it "no longer counts for us as the highest manner in which truth obtains existence for itself."[27] Heidegger traces the passing of art as carrier of truth to "the time when specialized thinking about art and the artist began," when aesthetics began to consider the work of art "an object…of sensuous apprehension in the wild sense. Today we call this apprehension experience. …Yet perhaps experience is the element in which art dies. The dying occurs so slowly that it takes a few centuries."[28]

Heidegger's disapproval of aesthetic thinking stems from its forced separation from truth. In his *Ister* lectures of the 1920s, he explains how logical positivists essentially "aestheticized" ethics by expelling ethics from the domain of truth-carrying thought, which for them is obtainable

---

24 Ibid., 79.
25 Jacques Taminiaux, "On Heidegger's Interpretation of the Will to Power as Art," in *New Nietzsche Studies*, Vol. 3, nos. 1 and 2 (1999): 2.
26 Heidegger, *OWA*, 78.
27 Hegel, *Lectures on Aesthetics,* quoted in Heidegger, *OWA*, 78.
28 Heidegger, *OWA*, 77.

exclusively by way of reason. Their account relegates ethics to the realm of feeling. Similarly, writes Julian Young, once "positivism aestheticizes art…cancel[ling] its truth-bearing function, all one is left with is its aesthetic function." While both Hegel and Heidegger recognize that aesthetic thinking has isolated art from the realm of reason, Hegel regards this as a positive development, but Heidegger does not.[29]

Even in speaking of the art of earlier historical periods, Hegel distinguishes in *LHP* between an "instinct of reason" and "thinking reason." Explaining why ancient Greek mythology must be excluded from the history of Philosophy, he seems to apply aesthetic thinking to his analysis, thus ignoring his own warning, repeated several times over the course of the Introduction to *LHP*, that "it is not historic when a theory unthought of by the ancients" is read into their thought.

> As the products of reason, though not of thinking reason…the mythologies, however simple and even foolish they may appear, indubitably contain as genuine works of art, thoughts, universal determinations and truth, for the instinct of reason is at their basis. …since mythology in its expression takes sensuous forms… [it is] of such a nature so as not to express the Idea. It…may undoubtedly contain something of the Idea in analogy, but the connection is far removed, and many contingent circumstances must find their entrance.[30]

Hegel then reiterates the distinction between potentiality and actuality, between "thoughts which are only implicite contained in some particular form or another" and thoughts that "come to consciousness in the form of Thought."[31] Hegel's admission that "as genuine works of art" the myths contain "thoughts, universal determinations and truth," taken together with his propositions on art as "the highest manner in which truth obtains existence for itself" and its form as "the highest need of the spirit,"[32] suggest that Hegel accepts these two conditions as intrinsic elements of art in earlier historical periods.

Hegel rejects art as an explicit coming of Thought to consciousness because of its sensuous form and contingent circumstances. The latter locate a historical group of people within a certain time and place—their culture, which Hegel enumerates as "all the customs, actions, furnishings, vestments, and offerings taken together."[33] Hegel attempts to filter out

---

29 Julian Young, *Heidegger's Philosophy of Art* (Cambridge: Cambridge University Press, 2001), 13–14.
30 Hegel, *LHP*, 82–83.
31 Ibid., 83.
32 Ibid., 82–83.
33 Ibid., 82–83.

these contingent circumstances, or what Heidegger refers to in *BT* as Dasein's factical existence (the *existentiell*).[34] Hegel limits the role of the history of Philosophy to tracing the development of consciousness, to dealing "with this development and bringing forth of thought." He argues that "every philosophy belongs to its own time and is restricted by its own limitations, just because it is the manifestation of a particular stage in development," and warns that "we are too apt to mold the ancient philosophers into our own forms of thought." He cites existing histories of Philosophy that ascribe views to an earlier philosopher "which he neither thought nor knew a word."[35]

Arguing for a unified philosophy of being, Heidegger was convinced that this separation between philosophy as worldview and philosophy as scientific in Hegel's Philosophy and other philosophies had ensured the failure of these philosophies as ontology.[36] It was precisely Hegel's interpretation of Greek concepts in terms of a later philosophical method, itself the product of a different worldview, that compelled Heidegger to assert that Hegel's account is internally flawed.

> When, from the perspective of absolute subjectivity, Hegel interprets being in a speculative and dialectical manner as the indeterminate immediate, the abstract universal, and explicates the basic words for being in Greek...within this horizon of modern philosophy, we are tempted to judge this explication to be historiographically incorrect.[37]

The basis of Heidegger's assertion is historical. Thinking in terms of the absolute subject is not for Hegel not a contingent circumstance, but rather a later development in the ascending movement of the stages of the history of Philosophy toward universal Truth. Even so, for Heidegger it still implies "a certain relation to history," one that presupposes that "Hegel experienced the essence of history in terms of the essence of being in the sense of absolute subjectivity."[38]

Heidegger's objection to Hegel's account of the history of Philosophy and the doctrine of being seems to be one of method. Because Hegel's speculative dialectic incorporates the Cartesian subject and takes universal Truth (the Idea) as its ultimate goal—and therefore not fully present in

---

34   Heidegger, *BT*, 12.
35   Hegel, *LHP*, 43–45.
36   Heidegger, *The Basic Problems of Phenomenology*, 10–15.
37   Heidegger, "Hegel and the Greeks," 333.
38   Ibid., 333.

earlier stages of philosophy—Hegel misses the possibility of truth *as* possibility.

> ...the speculative-dialectical determination of history does entail that it remained denied to Hegel to see Aletheia and its holding sway expressly as the matter of thinking, and this occurs in precisely that philosophy which determined "the realm of pure truth" to be "the goal" of philosophy. For, when Hegel conceives being as the indeterminate immediate, he experiences it as what is posited by the determining and conceiving subject. Accordingly, he is not able to release *einai*, being in the Greek sense, from the relation to the subject, and set it free into its own essence.[39]

Hegel's method conceals the fundamental ontology of aletheia as the disclosure of being because he understands "truth" not as unconcealedness, but—in Heidegger's words—as "the absolute certainty of the self-knowing absolute subject. But for the Greeks, according to his interpretation, the subject does not yet come to appearance *as* subject. Thus, Aletheia cannot be what determines truth in the sense of certainty."[40]

In the penultimate section of *BT*, Heidegger points out that Hegel's Interpretation of time, with its "monstrous privileging" of the "now," moves "wholly in the direction of the way time is ordinarily understood."[41] In "Hegel and the Greeks," Heidegger makes a similar point concerning Hegel's Interpretation of truth, namely that Hegel remains within a traditional, factical understanding of truth as certainty or agreement. This traditional understanding, as Heidegger explains in his discussion of truth in the final section of *BT* Division One, is the understanding of factical, everyday Dasein. Because of Dasein's Being-in-the-world, its lostness in the they of a world into which it is thrown, "that which has been uncovered and disclosed stands in a mode in which it has been disguised and closed off by idle talk, curiosity, and ambiguity. ... Entities...show themselves, but in the mode of semblance. Likewise, what has formerly been uncovered sinks back again, hidden and disguised."[42] This "sinking back" is a sign of the state of the factical falling essential to Dasein's everydayness. Hegel also uses a "sinking" motif in reference to the "ordinary consciousness" of any given historical group of people:

> the condition and culture of the time and of the people...consist mainly in the general ideas and aims, in the whole extent of the particular intellectual powers dominating consciousness and life. Our consciousness has these ideas and allows them to be considered ultimate determinations; it makes use of them as guiding and

---

39 Ibid., 333.
40 Ibid., 332; Heidegger's emphasis.
41 Heidegger, *BT*, 483 (431).
42 Ibid., 264–5.

> connecting links, but does not know them and does not even make them the objects of consideration... this web and its knots in our ordinary consciousness are sunk into a manifold material...[43]

In Heidegger's account, this traditional conception of truth is derived from the primordial phenomenon of truth. Hegel, in explaining the progress from implicit thought to Notion to Idea as explicitly determined thought (and ultimate Truth), also posits that Truth, is "our starting point...from which all proceeds", and everything leads "back to that single source."[44] But Heidegger seeks an authentic pre-philosophical antecedent to truth as certainty to fulfill his primordial conception of truth. In *BT* Division One, section 44, Heidegger introduces "Being-uncovering" as a "drastic" way of defining "Being-true," i.e., "truth." His definition primordially appropriates the traditional conception of truth as agreement or certainty. Heidegger proposes an understanding of truth as attaining to the uncoveredness of Being—bringing being out of hiding. He points out that even the translation of *logos* as truth "hides" the element of uncoveredness that "the Greeks made 'self-evidently' basic for the terminological use of *aletheia* as a pre-philosophical way of understanding [truth]."[45] In reference to the history of philosophy, Heidegger poses this elsewhere as a question, seemingly putting it to Hegel himself: "when we look through the entire history of philosophy, "Hegel and the Greeks," its completion and its beginning...does not Aletheia, truth, stand over the beginning of the path of philosophy?"[46]

The question turns on whether our way of being in the world allows us to see this primordial truth. This authentically truthful way of being is our own "uncoveredness." In *BT* Heidegger sets out the following ontological account of disclosedness as a kind of being essential to Dasein:

> Dasein, as constituted by disclosedness, is essentially in the truth. Disclosedness is a kind of Being which is essential to Dasein. *'There is' truth only in so far as Dasein i s and so long as Dasein i s.* Entities are uncovered only when Dasein *is*; and only as long as Dasein *is*, are they disclosed. ...Once entities have been uncovered, they show themselves precisely as entities which beforehand already were. Such uncovering is the kind of Being which belongs to 'truth.'[47]

As its authentic disclosedness, *"Dasein is 'in the truth.'"* But Dasein is

---

43 Hegel, *LHP*, 29.
44 Ibid., 19–20.
45 Heidegger, *BT*, 262.
46 Heidegger, "Hegel and the Greeks," 331–2.
47 Heidegger, *BT*, 269; Heidegger's emphasis.

also in *untruth*. That Dasein's Being-in-the-world can be "equiprimordially both in the truth and in untruth" is explained ontologically by Dasein's thrown projection.[48] In *OWA* Heidegger treats this unity of truth/untruth in more Hegelian terms, as a negation and as a "double-concealment."

The Work of Art as Illuminating Projection

In *OWA* Heidegger further develops the idea of truth as disclosedness through his concept of the Open:

> In referring to this self-establishing of openness in the Open... [it] should be noted, that if the nature of the unconcealedness of beings belongs in any way to Being itself... then Being, by way of its own nature, lets the place of openness (the lighting-clearing of the There) happen, and introduces it as a place of the sort in which each being emerges or arises in its own way.[49]

The work of art initiates this lighting or clearing of the Open as a unity of two motions. An intersubjective "happening of truth" allows those who stand within the clearing—the preservers of the work of art (a historical group of people)—to see in a way they have not seen before. Heidegger speaks of disclosedness and the Open in terms of **lighting, motion,** and **language.**

Lighting. Heidegger links seeing to lighting, making sustained use of what I call his "light motif."[50] Also found in *BT*, the Heideggerian light motif runs throughout *OWA*, from Heidegger's description of the happening of truth in a Greek temple to his characterization of poetry as "illuminating projection." These examples illustrate how the previously unseen is revealed—made seeable, brought into the light of the Open (the clearing, *Lichtung*)[51]—by the work of art. Those who are encircled in the Open join in the knowing, sharing it with the artist. The resulting "increase in being" for the participants is not "made to happen"— its happening is outside the control of those who share in it.

In reference to ancient Greek philosophy and specifically to Plato, Heidegger had previously asserted that "any seeing is already, and above

---

48 Ibid., 263–5; Heidegger's emphasis.
49 Heidegger, *OWA*, 59.
50 I have indulged in a play on words with *leitmotiv* (a leading or recurring musical idea) famously used by Richard Wagner in his *Ring* cycle.
51 Thomas Sheehan, "Dasein," in *A Companion to Heidegger*, ed. H. Dreyfus and M. Wrathall (Blackwell, 2005), 201 (see "4"—the opening that clarifies things).

all, related to the light."⁵² He observed something similar in Aristotle's account of human learning, which, according to Kisiel and Sheehan's commentary on Heidegger's 1922 lectures on Aristotle, "progresses by way of the comparatives of "seeing more," "knowing more," and "wiser," until one arrives at the apex of wisdom in knowing or "seeing" and so "understanding the ultimate "aspects" of the "look" of things, which turn out to be their first "whence.""⁵³

In terms of the facticity of everyday ontic Dasein, Heidegger's light motif seems to belong to his conception of the everyday understanding and use of "datable" time. This datability has to do with how time makes itself public to Dasein for Being-in-the-world, as Heidegger explains in the following passage from *BT*, in which the possibility of sight and the presence of brightness in the world are intrinsically linked:

> Everyday circumspective Being-in-the-world needs the *possibility of sight* (and this means that it needs brightness) if it is to deal concernfully with what is ready-to-hand within the present-to-hand. With the factical disclosedness of Dasein's world, Nature has been uncovered for Dasein. In its thrownness Dasein has been surrendered to the changes of day and night. Day with its brightness gives it the possibility of sight; night takes it away.
> ... Concern makes use of the 'Being-ready-to-hand' of the sun, which sheds forth light and warmth. The sun dates the time which is interpreted in concern. In terms of this dating arises the 'most natural' measure of time—the day.
> ... Dasein historicizes *from day to day* by reason of its way of interpreting time by dating it—a way which is adumbrated in its thrownness into the "there." This dating of things in terms of the heavenly body which sheds forth light and warmth, and in terms of its distinctive 'places' in the sky, is a way of assigning time which can be done in our Being with one another 'under the same sky,' and which can be done for 'Everyman' at any time in the same way, so that within certain limits everyone is agreed upon it."⁵⁴

Earlier in *BT* Heidegger establishes *circumspection* as the kind of seeing that is a "guide for practical concern," and speaks of it in terms of light:

> Circumspective deliberation illumines Dasein's current factical situation in the environment with which it concerns itself. ...Bringing the environment closer in circumspective deliberation has the existential meaning of a *making present*; for *envisaging* is only a mode of this. In envisaging, one's deliberation catches sight

---

52   Martin Heidegger, *Basic Concepts of Ancient Philosophy*, trans. R. Rojcewicz (Bloomington: Indiana University Press, 2007), 117.
53   Martin Heidegger, *Becoming Heidegger*, ed. T. Kisiel and T. Sheehan (Evanston: Northwestern University Press, 2007), 182.
54   Heidegger, BT, 465–6 (412–3); Heidegger's emphasis.

directly of that which is needed but is un-ready-to-hand. Circumspection which envisages does not relate itself to 'mere representations.'[55]

Circumspective deliberation plays an important role in interpretation—in seeing *as*, where the *as* is also grounded in ecstatic-horizonal unity of temporality.

In the section of *BT* entitled "The Temporality of Being-in-the-world and the Problem of the Transcendence of the World,"[56] which I take to be an interpretation of Hegel's internal/external dialectic, Heidegger discusses the ontological significance of "light" as the essential—not merely momentary—clearedness, as a basic condition for understanding. The ecstatical unity of temporality allows this clearedness to happen.

> The ecstatical unity of temporality—that is, the unity of the 'outside-of-itself' in the raptures of the future, of what has been, and of the Present—is the condition for the possibility that there can be an entity which exists as its 'there.' The entity which bears the title "Being-there" [i.e., Dasein] is one that has been 'cleared.' The light which constitutes this clearedness of Dasein, is not something ontically present-at-hand as power or source for a radiant brightness occurring in the entity on occasion. That by which this entity is essentially cleared—in other words, that which makes it both 'open' for itself and 'bright' for itself—is what we have defined as "care," in advance of any 'temporal' Interpretation. In care is grounded the disclosedness of the "there." **Only by this clearedness is any illuminating or illumining, any awareness, 'seeing,' or having of something, made possible.** We understand the light of this clearedness only if we are not seeking some power implanted in us and present-at-hand, but are interrogating the whole constitution of Dasein's Being—namely, care—and are interrogating is as to the unitary basis for its existential possibility. ***Ecstatical temporality clears the "there" primordially.*** It is what primarily regulates the possible unity of all Dasein's existential structures.[57]

In *OWA* Heidegger references the light motif as he elaborates on clearedness (unconcealedness) in terms of the Open. Here he attempts to explain "more clearly what this unconcealedness itself is."

> Things are, and human beings...are. ...And yet—beyond what is...an open place occurs. There is a clearing, a lighting. ...The lighting center itself encircles all that is, like the Nothing which we scarcely know. ...That which is can only be, as a being, if it stands within and stands out within what is lighted in this clearing.[58]

The Open, the open place beyond being, beyond what is, is the ultimate

---

55 Ibid., 410–11 (359–60); Heidegger's emphasis.
56 Ibid., 401–18.
57 Heidegger, *BT*, 401–2; my bold emphasis (Italics original).
58 Heidegger, *OWA*, 51.

condition for being. This condition is encapsulated by *Ereignis*,[59] the key word of Heidegger's later philosophy. As Thomas Sheehan puts it, "being is embedded within Ereignis...because Ereignis is the ultimate source of all the various dispensations of being." This "openedness" can only occur if we are conditioned to be receptive to it, only "with and as Da-sein, our a priori opened-ness." In this connection Sheehan argues for an alternative translation of Dasein (usually translated as "being there") as "being-the-open," explaining that "Heidegger, both early and late, holds that the human essence consists in necessarily (=a priori) being the Da. Dasein = "being-the-open" in the double sense of "always already having been opened" and "having to be that already-opened-ness.""[60]

The light shining forth in Heidegger's work of art does not illuminate the earth, because its light emanates from the earth itself. As Hegel writes of the Idea, it is "the source of light, which in all its expansion does not come without itself, but remains present and immanent within itself."[61] Heidegger, using the example of a Greek temple, explains how a work of art "opens up a world and at the same time sets this world back again on earth, which itself only thus emerges as native ground." The presence of the work of art exposes the possibility of a new world in relation to the existing world. Heidegger offers a particularly poetic description of this clearing of the Open that also points to his recurring characterizations of the moment of vision—of circumspective seeing—as a "coming into the light":

> The luster and gleam of the stone [of the temple], though itself apparently glowing only by the grace of the sun, yet first brings to light the light of the day, the breadth of the sky, the darkness of the night. The temple's firm towering makes visible the invisible space of air. The steadfastness of the work contrasts with the surge of the surf, and its own repose brings out the raging of the sea. Tree and grass, eagle and bull, snake and cricket first enter into their distinctive shapes and thus come to appear as what they are.[62]

This passage also makes poetic reference to a unity of motions and to the

---

59 Thomas Sheehan discusses the difficulties of an adequate English translation of Ereignis in "Facticity and Ereignis," in *Interpreting Heidegger: New Essays*, ed. D. Dahlstrom (Cambridge: Cambridge University Press, 2011), 52–60. Sheehan: "Heidegger refuses the usual, non-technical translation of Ereignis as "event" and interprets it instead as the appropriation of man to the meaning-giving process." (53) "The man-meaning relation—Ereignis—is one of co-equal reciprocity." (57)
60 Thomas Sheehan, "Being, Opened-ness, and Unlimited Technology: Ten Theses on Heidegger," *PortiQue: Revue de philosophie et de sciences humaines* (18: 2006): 1256.
61 Hegel, *LHP*, 28.
62 Heidegger, *OWA*, 41.

repose/motion dialectic, discussed on the following pages.

Motion. Illuminating projection can also be understood in terms of forward motion. Referring to origins or new beginnings, Heidegger characterizes this projection as "a founding leap[:] a genuine beginning, as a leap, is always a head start."[63] As such, this projection can be tied to *BT* concepts such the authentic futurity of the ecstatical unity of temporal horizons and to Dasein's historicality. Because of tradition, Dasein is always factically ahead of itself. In positing the happening of art as a beginning in a historical sense, Heidegger refers obliquely to ecstatical unity in relation to the ordinary conception of time:

> Whenever art happens—that is, whenever there is a beginning—a thrust enters history, history either begins or starts over again. History means here not a sequence in time of events of whatever sort, however important. History is the transporting of a people into its appointed task as entrance into that people's endowment.[64]

For Heidegger, an origin is a way that "truth comes into being, that is, becomes historical." But the happening of truth in art is directed toward the future—when it happens, it is already in motion: "in the work, truth is thrown toward the coming preservers, that is, toward a historical group of [people]."[65] In contrast, when Hegel speaks of history of Philosophy, he privileges the present and the "products of reason [that] form the content of this history" as "not past," and the True as being true "beyond all time"— "the history of Philosophy has not to do with what is gone, but with the living present."[66]

In *BT*, Heidegger compares the historicality of authentic and inauthentic Dasein, discussing it in terms of a specific type of movement. Heidegger calls this movement a "stretching-along" that happens "within the horizon of Dasein's temporal constitution."[67] Heidegger's ontological explication of how Dasein "stretches along between birth and death" moves beyond the ordinary interpretation of Dasein, which he has worked out in *BT* by positing temporality as the meaning of the Being of care. The ordinary interpretation regards the connectedness of life as a succession of Experiences, where "only the Experience one is having 'right now' is 'actual'" and birth and death are conceived as the outer boundaries of a framework in which these Experiences occur. The ontological

---

63   Ibid., 73.
64   Ibid., 74.
65   Ibid., 73.
66   Hegel, *LHP*, 39.
67   Heidegger, *BT*, 427.

Interpretation of the Being between birth and death reveals that

> Dasein does not fill up a track or stretch of 'life'—one which is somehow present-at-hand—with the phases of its momentary activities. It stretches itself along in such a way that its own Being is constituted in advance as a stretching-along. The 'between' which relates to birth and death already lies in the Being of Dasein.

The "connectedness of life" is not something external to Dasein—it comes from within and is primordially grounded. Heidegger believes that this is something that Dasein in its average everydayness intuitively understands: "even in the ordinary way of taking the 'connectedness of life,' one does not think of...a framework drawn tense 'outside' of Dasein and spanning it round, but one rightly seeks this connectedness within Dasein itself."[68]

Heidegger's ontological explanation of how Dasein stretches itself along draws support from his conception of a unity of temporal horizons—the ecstatico-temporal unity referred to earlier. This conception is essentially different from the ordinary linear conception of time in terms of past-present-future and a succession of nows:

> Understood existentially, birth is not and never is something past in the sense of something no longer present-at-hand; and death is just as far from having the kind of Being of something still outstanding, not yet present-at-hand but coming along. Factical Dasein exists as born; and, as born, it is already dying, in the sense of Being-towards-death. As long as Dasein factically exists, both the 'ends' and their 'between' are, and they are in the only way which is possible on the basis of Dasein's Being as care. Thrownness and that Being towards death in which one either flees it or anticipates it, form a unity; and in this unity birth and death are 'connected' in a manner characteristic of Dasein. As care, Dasein is the 'between.'[69]

Dasein's temporality is the basis not only of its Being of care, but also of its essential historicality. In his existential Interpretation of Dasein's historicality, Heidegger finds his progress hampered by "the enigma of Being, and...of motion." But he also asserts that "the very aim of this exposition is to lead us face to face with the ontological enigma of the movement of historizing in general." Because the historizing of history is the historizing of Being-in-the-world, "Dasein's historicality is essentially the historicality of the world, which, on the basis of ecstatico-horizonal temporality, belongs to the temporalizing of that temporality... entities within-the-world are historical as such, and their history does not signify something 'external' which merely accompanies the 'inner' history of the 'soul.'" Heidegger's attempt to capture the "character of movement"

---

68 Ibid., 426.
69 Ibid., 427.

of "the *world-historical*"—entities within the world—makes clear that he is not talking about motion as a change of location: "history is neither the connectedness of motions in the alterations of Objects, nor a free-floating sequence of Experiences which 'subjects' have had."[70]

The true character of this movement is linked to the constituents of Dasein's authentic historicality—fate and repetition. In our inauthenticity we seek to establish connectedness in the present-at-hand Experiences of a subject, from "the *dispersion* and *disconnectedness* of the very things that have 'come to pass.'" This places the burden on Dasein to "think up for itself a unity" and conceals how "the whole of existence stretched along in [authentic] historicality...has no need of connectedness." Whereas inauthentic historicality reflects a lostness in the they that Heidegger has revealed as "a fleeing in the face of death," authentic historicality is the historizing of the anticipatory resoluteness that "brings this Being-towards-death into authentic existence."[71] Heidegger speaks of something similar in reference to the Greek temple, which "gathers around itself the unity of those paths and relations in which birth and death, disaster and blessing, victory and disgrace, endurance and decline acquire the shape of destiny for human being."[72]

Because the "unconcealedness of beings...is never a merely existent state, but a happening,"[73] Heidegger conceives of the happening of truth in the work of art in terms of a unity of two types of motion: the setting up of a world and the setting forth of earth. The state of unified repose that we sense in a work of art is, in Heidegger's account, the resolution of a struggle between earth and world that the work of art sets into motion. Historically, this setting into motion is an origin. As the happening of truth as unconcealedness, it is the clearing of a space—the Open. Heidegger characterizes this struggle in terms of "the primal conflict,"

> in which... the Open is won within which everything stands and from which everything withholds itself that shows itself and withdraws itself as a being. Whenever and however this conflict breaks out and happens, the opponents, lighting or clearing and concealing, move apart because of it. Thus the Open of the place of conflict is won. The openness of this open, that is, truth, can be what it is, namely, *this* openness, only if and as long as it establishes itself within its Open.[74]

---

70 Ibid., 440–4; Heidegger's emphasis.
71 Ibid., 441–2; Heidegger's emphasis.
72 Heidegger, *OWA*, 41.
73 Ibid., 52.
74 Ibid., 58–59; Heidegger's emphasis.

A unity of motions is also central to Hegel's conception of the development of the concrete as the path toward the perfect Philosophy. In Hegel's motion of the concrete, "the going without itself of development also is a going inwards." Similarly to the earth in Heidegger's account, the Hegelian universal Idea "continues to remain at the foundation and still is the all-embracing and unchangeable." Like the self-concealing earth, the Idea itself is both "central point" and "periphery." Hegel states that "what is true is...found in motion, in a process, however, in which there is rest; difference, while it lasts, is but a temporary condition; through which comes unity, full and concrete."[75] The motion of the concrete makes difference distinguishable.

In Heidegger's account of the work of art, the unity of the "state of movement" is one where "the repose of the work...rests in itself." Because rest is "only the limiting case of motion...there can exist a repose which is an inner concentration of motion, hence a highest state of agitation."[76] This allows the initiation of struggle and its resolution to happen together. Heidegger illustrates this unity of motions poetically in the Greek temple passage: the temple "opens up a world and at the same time sets this world back again on earth."[77]

Heidegger's concept of repose as "an inner concentration of motion" seems to be inspired by Aristotle's doctrine of motion and rest.[78] Heidegger's engagement with this doctrine can be traced at least as far back as his 1922 course on "Phenomenological Interpretations Relating to Aristotle: Ontology and Logic," where Heidegger refers specifically to two Aristotelian concepts of motion: chance and spontaneity. According to Keiler and Sheehan, both of these concepts "probe deeply into the "happening" of history and thus come closest to characterizing the thoroughly historical movement of factic human life in the midst of beings which "also can be otherwise.""[79] Heidegger's reading of Aristotle's definition of motion as an equating of *kinêsis* with *energeia*—Heidegger refers to them collectively as "active potentiality"—is said to have to have helped him shape his description of Dasein as in terms of motion and "movedness."[80]

---

75 Hegel, *LHP*, 25.
76 Heidegger, *OWA*, 47.
77 Ibid., 41.
78 Joseph J. Kockelmans, *Heidegger on Art and Art Works* (The Hague: Martinus Nijhoff, 1985), 154.
79 *Becoming Heidegger*, 183.
80 Joseph P. Carter, "Heidegger's Sein zum Tode as radicalization of Aristotle's definition of kinêsis," *Epoché: A Journal for the History of Philosophy*, 18.2 (2014): 473–502.

He emphasizes the Aristotelian idea that "where motion is[,] experienced time is unveiled," and when he begins his discussion in *BT* of Hegel's understanding of the relation between Time and Spirit, Heidegger acknowledges Aristotle as having undertaken the first "thematically detailed traditional interpretation" of time, in which time, location, and movement "are taken together."[81] In his own ontological Interpretation, Heidegger delimits the movement of "happening" from "motion as change of location" and treats it as a kind of Being when he addresses "the ontological enigma of the movement of historicizing." [82]

Language. Illuminating projection is also the "projective saying" of poetry. In *OWA* Heidegger declares that all art, "as the letting happen of the advent of the truth of what is, is, as such, essentially poetry." As illuminating projection, "poetry...projects ahead," letting happen "the Open [that] brings beings to shine and ring out." Heidegger grants that all arts operate in various modes of "the lighting projection of truth, i.e., of poetic composition in [the] wider sense [of poesy]," but gives "the linguistic work, the poem in the narrower sense...a privileged position in the domain of the arts."[83]

Heidegger's explanation of poetry as "projective saying" brings together several threads of his thought: his then-new conceptions of the fourfold and of the conflict of world and earth are related to unconcealedness as the arising of the unfamiliar from the midst of the familiar and ordinary. "The working of the work...lies in a change... of Being." Speaking in terms of origin as new beginning, Heidegger relates "the happening of this saying" to "a people's world historically aris[ing] for it. In such saying, the concepts of a people's historical nature, i.e., of its belonging to world history, are formed for that folk, before it."[84]

Heidegger offers a historical succession of three worlds initiated by art: Greek, Christian, and Modern. This succession seems to resemble Hegel's ascending historical stages in the development of Philosophy. However, although Heidegger still speaks in terms of transformation, the Hegelian element of dialectic incorporation has been transposed into "the instigation of the strife of truth"—the momentary conflict of self-concealing Earth and the arising, disclosed World that art both initiates and

---

81 Heidegger, *BT*, 481.
82 Ibid., 441.
83 Heidegger, *OWA*, 70–71.
84 Ibid., 70–71.

resolves. This conflict is an establishing, and the Greek world "sets the standard":

> Always when that which is as a whole demands, as what is, itself, a grounding in openness, art attains to its historical nature as foundation. This foundation happened in the West for the first time in Greece. What was in the future to be called Being was set into the work, setting the standard. The realm of beings thus opened up was then transformed into a being in the sense of God's creation. This happened in the Middle Ages. This kind of being was again transformed at the beginning and in the course of the modern age. Beings became objects that could controlled and seen through by calculation. **At each time a new and essential world arose.** At each time the openness of what is had to be established in beings themselves, by the fixing in place of truth in figure. At each time there happened unconcealedness of what is. Unconcealedness sets itself into work, a setting which is accomplished by art.[85]

In *OWA* Heidegger incisively illustrates the parallel powers of language to disclose being—by bringing a new world into appearance—and to conceal being in the self-concealing earth. He brings this contrast itself into appearance through his use of overtly poetic language when he discusses the examples of the peasant shoes (in Van Gogh's painting) and the Greek temple. Interpreted as art, these passages can in themselves be said to show how art is an origin when truth is understood as unconcealedness. "When truth sets itself into the work, it appears. Appearance—as this being of truth in the work and as work—is beauty. Thus the beautiful belongs to the advent of truth."[86] In this way Heidegger reasserts the unity of truth and beauty as aletheia.

Heidegger contrasts these poetic passages with ones discussing processes of concealment of meaning through "seemingly literal and thus faithful translation," where history is seen in terms of human facticity—Dasein's being in "untruth." Rather than accruing in a Hegelian succession of historical stages, meanings are hidden and potentially lost in a process that started "with the appropriation of Greek words by Roman-Latin thought…without a corresponding, equally authentic experience of what they say, without the Greek word."

By concealing "the basic Greek experience of the Being of beings in the sense of presence,"[87] truth and beauty became separated. In the final paragraph of the epilogue, and with specific reference to the words by which concepts were made known, Heidegger succinctly traces the steps

---

85 Ibid., 74; my emphasis.
86 Ibid., 79.
87 Ibid., 23.

by which the unity of beauty with truth became concealed, again through Greek-to-Latin *trans*lation:

> The beautiful belongs to the advent of truth, truth's taking of its place. It does not exist merely relative to pleasure and purely as its object. The beautiful does lie in form, but only because the *forma* once took its light from Being as the isness of what is. Being at that time made its advent as *eidos*. The idea fits itself into the *morphe*. The *sunolon*, the unitary whole of *morphe* and *hule*, namely the *ergon*, is in the manner of *energeia*. This mode of presence becomes the *actualitas* of the *ens actu*. The *actualitas* becomes reality. Reality becomes objectivity. Objectivity becomes experience. In the way in which, for the world determined by the West, that which is, is as the real, there is concealed a peculiar confluence of beauty with truth.

Heidegger concludes that "the history of the nature of Western art corresponds to the change of the nature of truth." It is precisely this change that allows Hegel to posit—incorrectly in Heidegger's view, because he applied a later understanding of truth—that in the history of Philosophy, the stage of Greek philosophy is "the stage of the beautiful," and as such it has not attained the level of truth. Truth has become scientifically objective "in the sense of certainty," and is "that which is generally recognized under the name and assigned to cognition and science as a quality in order to distinguish from it the beautiful and the good, which function as names for the values of non-theoretical activities."[88]

Heidegger declares in *BT* that "the ultimate business of philosophy is to preserve *the force of the most elemental words* in which Dasein expresses itself, and to keep the common understanding from leveling them off to that unintelligibility which functions in turn as a source of pseudo-problems."[89] In *OWA* he has identified just such a source, stemming from a loss of force, a leveling off that over time hides the meaning—the original truth—of these words.

Reclaiming the Happening of Truth

I return now to Heidegger's question: "is art still an essential and necessary way in which that truth happens which is decisive for our historical existence…"?[90] Hubert L. Dreyfus proposes three possible ontological functions of the Heideggerian work of art: "for Heidegger, an artwork is a thing that, when it works…either manifests, articulates or reconfigures the

---

88 Ibid., 79.
89 Heidegger, *BT* section 44, 262 (220); Heidegger's emphasis.
90 Heidegger, *OWA*, 78.

style of a culture from within the world of that culture."[91] Addressing Heidegger's question by reference to the explicitly social orientation of specific musical works of the American twentieth century, I in turn find three specific traits, each corresponding to one of Dreyfus' ontological functions: these works represent a **gathering of participants**, a **documentation of events**, or a non-dogmatic **prophesizing of future needs or outcomes**.

The musical art of the period immediately leading up to *OWA* can be characterized by its conflicted relationship to the music of the past. Introduced just before World War I, the twelve-tone compositional system of Schoenberg was both a radical way forward from the then seemingly exhausted possibilities of Romantic musical style and a logical extension of this style, out of which it grew. Neoclassicism emerged at about the same time as composers such as Prokofiev and Stravinsky tried to bypass Romantic musical traditions by referencing—at times reverently, at others satirically—stylistic features of music from the eighteenth century.

In this context, Heidegger would likely have appreciated the efforts of American composers during the twentieth century to break with the mainstream musical traditions in various ways, especially because in doing so they were often consciously connecting with their own way of being in the world. Charles Ives unabashedly used quotations from non-classical music that he had grown up with in his hometown, recreating in his compositions specific sound phenomena as he had heard them. Harry Partch spoke of a return to the ethos of ancient Greece and recapturing greater sensitivity to subtle shades of pitch that had been gradually hidden since the introduction of tempered tuning during the Enlightenment; Partch supported his ideas with a unique microtonal scale of forty-three pitches to the octave (compare to the traditional twelve) and musical instruments of his own design and construction. John Cage turned to Eastern philosophy (Zen Buddhism and the *I-Ching*) as he eschewed the traditional control that a composer had over what constitutes the work of art: aleatoric, or chance, music was the result, giving more control to the performer and inviting the listener to experience all sounds—not just those created and manipulated by the performer—as having musical interest. The social inclusiveness of Cage's approach is suggested by his concept of a "happening," where the music consists of whatever happens among all

---

91   Hubert L. Dreyfus, "Heidegger on Art" (2008), unpublished manuscript, http://sophos.berkeley.edu/dreyfus/ (last accessed January 24, 2015). Quoted with permission from the author.

participants during a specified period of time in a given space. In the 1950s Morton Feldman, a younger composer in Cage's New York circle, seems to have recognized a kind of Heideggerian new beginning—art as a "thrust entering history"—when he wrote of their total preoccupation during that decade with sound itself:

> For ten years of my life [we] worked...not knowing where what we did belonged, or whether it belonged anywhere at all. What we did was not in protest against the past. To rebel against history is still to be a part of it. We simply were not concerned with historical processes. We were concerned with sound itself. And sound does not know its history.[92]

A Gathering of Participants. To paraphrase Heidegger's statement on the history of philosophy from the introduction to *The Basic Problems of Phenomenology*, each of the above-mentioned examples illustrates music *being thought anew* rather than being completed à la Hegel.[93] Heidegger's conception of the "createdness" of the work of art as embracing (in an interpretation of the Greek *techne* as a mode of knowing rather than making) both artist and those who preserve the work of art, seems to anticipate the evolution of what constitutes a work of art. Its emphasis on the Open as a gathering allows us to understand John Cage's conception of a "happening," with its explicit dimension as a social gathering of (it might be supposed) like-minded people, as a kind of playing out in real time of Heidegger's "happening of truth." It likely inspired Gadamer to think more specifically of the "hermeneutic identity" of a work of art that relies on being performed—a music composition, a theatre or dance productions—as something achieved *only* through its actual performance, through the serious "playing together" of all participants, where all roles—performer, listener, etc.—are regarded as equally "co-active."[94]

A Documentation of Events. Charles Mingus and Steve Reich were among the well-known participants in the American music scene of the 1960s who insisted on music's social relevance at this pivotal period in United States history, at the height of the Civil Rights movement. The free jazz improvisations of the Charles Mingus Sextet and the early tape

---

92 Morton Feldman, *The Music of Morton Feldman*, ed. T. DeLio (Oxford: Psychology Press, 1996), 206.
93 See Heidegger, *The Basic Problems of Phenomenology*.
94 See Hans-Georg Gadamer, *The Relevance of the Beautiful and Other Essays*, trans. N. Walker, ed. R. Bernasconi (Cambridge: Cambridge University Press, 1986). Gadamer's conception of the hermeneutic identity is discussed further in Chapter 2.

compositions of Steve Reich can be read as musical reimaginings of the social status quo.

Mingus' composition *Meditations on Integration* metaphorically achieves, or least rehearses, racial integration by achieving its form and content through the contrasting improvisations of six jazz musicians brought together by Mingus precisely because of their diverse individual playing styles. Mingus' goal was to "integrate" these individuals in a musical whole.[95] Reich's composition *Come Out* was one of the earliest to employ a looping technique to generate a musical composition. By using a recording of a sentence spoken by an African American participant injured in the 1964 Harlem riots, Reich ensures the work's lasting value as documentary. But the form of the work "happens" as the natural result of two open-reel tape recorders playing the same sentence simultaneously and gradually becoming out of sync with each other. As Reich himself explained in 1968, the composer's role in this "music as a gradual process" is confined to lining up the two recordings and pressing the start buttons: "once the process is set up and loaded it runs by itself," resulting in "pieces of music that are, literally, processes."[96]

Reich and other so-called minimalist composers such as Philip Glass and John Adams have brought a heightened social consciousness to their music, turning again and again to the most troubling social themes of the twentieth century. In creating compositions in which "the documentary reality and the musical reality become one and the same,"[97] Reich has developed what he calls speech melodies, where the vocal inflections of recorded interviewees provide the melodic and rhythmic patterns, and he has used this technique in works that deal with the Holocaust, atomic bomb testing, cloning, etc., more recently with the help of a digital sampler. In several such projects (*Three Tales, The Cave*) he has collaborated with his wife, video artist Beryl Korot. The operas of John Adams also take actual events, such as Nixon's historic visit to China, the invention of the atomic bomb, a terrorist attack on a cruise ship, or a tsunami-like natural disaster, as their subjects. Philip Glass' large-scale works often center on "larger-than-life" historical figures of the twentieth century, such as Albert Einstein and Mahatma Gandhi.

---

95   Rob Bowman, liner notes to *Jazz Icons: Charles Mingus* (Naxos DVD, 2007).
96   Steve Reich, "Music as a Gradual Process," in *Writings on Music*, ed. P. Hillier (Oxford: Oxford University Press, 2002), 34.
97   Steve Reich, in reference to his composition *Different Trains* (1988), on The South Bank Show (UK, 2006), https://youtu.be/BhQfggqNuYM (last accessed February 7, 2015).

A Prophesizing of Future Needs or Outcomes. The personalities and issues of twentieth century life are also at the heart of some of the most substantial compositions of Philip Glass. In the three films of the *Qatsi* trilogy, he and director Godfrey Reggio created epic "film symphonies" on a previously unimagined scale. Made between 1975 and 1982, the first film is completely non-narrative, save the quasi-ritualistic unison choral intonations of its title, *Koyaanisqatsi*, a Hopi Indian word meaning "life out of balance" or "a way of life that calls for another way of life." It offers an epic vision of the discord between the natural world and human technology, and it seems to argue for a return to a kind of Heideggerian pre-technological world. The images of human-precipitated destruction, either actual (the explosion of a nuclear bomb or the space-shuttle Challenger) or possible (the ominous arial views of nuclear power plants and skyscrapers, the latter having new symbolic significance in a post-9/11 world), suggest an ever-present danger inherent in the way that humans—particularly in an advanced capitalistic culture—conduct their everyday business. The frenetic central episode of *Koyaanisqatsi*, distantly reminiscent of Charlie Chaplin's accelerated assembly-line in *Modern Times*, turns the individual faces seen earlier in the film into a churning mass of anonymous urban humanity funneling through the exits of mass transportation stations at impossible speeds and working rhythmically in factories to produce products for mass consumption. It is as if Heidegger's concern for the reduction of human beings to just another technological resource has found its ultimate expression.[98]

If *Koyaanisqatsi* argues for a return to a pre-technological world, or at least for "another way of life," these arguments are only implied: there is no producer-provided "owner's manual" for the interpretation of the film's message. Director Reggio insists that the film has no "predetermined meaning," stating that "the film's role is to provoke, to raise questions that only the audience can answer. This is the highest value of any work of art, not predetermined meaning, but meaning gleaned from the experience of the encounter."[99] The film's apparently anti-technological stance has led it to be labeled "Heideggerian,"[100] but I do not think it can be stated unequivocally that the film is anti-technological. The factory owner watching the scenes of "technology at work" in rhythm with Glass'

---

98 Martin Heidegger, "The Question of Technology" (1954).
99 Godfrey Reggio, note on *Koyaanisqatsi* http://www.koyaanisqatsi.org/aboutus/godfrey.php (last accessed February 2, 2015).
100 C.f. Bert Olivier, *Philosophy and the Arts: Collected Essays* (Peter Lang, 2009).

epic soundtrack could easily offer them as evidence that "technology *does* work," and scenes showing potential or actual disaster could be said to simply depict some of the unfortunate side effects of—or to use the well-worn cliché, the price that must be paid for—progress. But *Koyaanisqatsi* certainly gives rise to sobering thoughts about technology, and it very literally offers "another perspective" on the human relationship to the natural world, using time-lapse and panoramic cinematic techniques to an extent unheard of before this film was made to allow us to "see" everything from mountain chains to skyscrapers in a new way. The result is a grandeur of vision that is as awe-inspiring as it is unsettling. Ironically, it was technological progress that made this work of art possible.

Chapter 2

Dewey and Gadamer: Art as Community of Experience

The resonances of John Dewey's *Art as Experience* with the aesthetics of the German hermeneutic philosopher Hans-Georg Gadamer are striking. With differing emphases on usefulness and universality, each philosopher develops a comprehensive program of reunifying art with fundamental human experience. While expressing themselves in divergent terms, both Dewey and Gadamer conceive of continuity in terms of continuous movement, within a single experience and over broad temporal expanses. Perhaps most significantly, both single out art as a properly philosophical area of inquiry, thus underscoring its potential to serve as a critique of foundational Philosophy and the claims its proponents make for a higher Truth and the means of attaining it.

One obvious difference between these two thinkers, one that might be suspected at first to imply conflicting views on aesthetics, is where each of them stands within the main traditions of philosophy. John Dewey (1859–1952), together with William James, was a founder of philosophical pragmatism in the United States. Hans-Georg Gadamer (1900–2002) is one of the central hermeneutic philosophers in the continental tradition stemming from Martin Heidegger in Germany. Dewey's major work on aesthetics is *Art as Experience*, published in 1934, and first presented as a series of ten lectures at Harvard University in 1931.[1] Gadamer treats aesthetics at length in the first part of *Truth and Method*[2] of 1960 and returns to it in his extended essay "The Relevance of the Beautiful."[3]

Richard Shusterman has identified "considerable areas of overlap between Dewey's thought and [continental] traditions."[4] In addition, while

---

1. John Dewey, *Art as Experience* (New York: Perigee, 1934). Referred to in subsequent footnotes as *AE*.
2. Hans-Georg Gadamer, *Truth and Method*, trans. J. Weinsheimer and D. Marshall (New York: Crossroad, 1992).
3. Hans-Georg Gadamer, *The Relevance of the Beautiful and Other Essays*, trans. N. Walker, ed. R. Bernasconi (Cambridge: Cambridge University Press, 1986). Referred to in subsequent footnotes as *RB*.
4. Richard Shusterman, "Pragmatism Between Aesthetic Experience and Aesthetic Education," *Studies in Philosophy and Education*, Vol. 22, no. 5 (2003): 404.

focusing on areas of difference between Dewey and Gadamer, John Gilmore invokes Richard Rorty's championing of Dewey's anti-foundational philosophy as Heideggerian and finds that "much of [Dewey's] treatment of art is close to historicist approaches among Continental thinkers."[5] Rorty[6] and Jürgen Habermas[7] have noted that both pragmatic and continental philosophers of the twentieth century have challenged the authority and ability of foundationalist Philosophy to find a "better" truth or definitive answers to the perennial questions of knowledge and morals.

Two Anti-Foundational Approaches to Aesthetics

Dewey's dual allegiance to evolutionary naturalism and scientific method differentiates his philosophy from the continental tradition.[8] A marked utilitarian strain can be discerned in his aesthetics, which emphasize the usefulness of art to human purposes. The contours of Dewey's pragmatism quickly emerge in *Art as Experience* as he develops his ideas in terms of human needs and how we interact with our environment. The following is a characteristic example:

> The man who poked the sticks of burning wood would say he did it to make the fire burn better; but he is none the less fascinated by the colorful drama of change enacted before his eyes and imaginatively partakes of it. He does not remain a cold spectator.[9]

For Dewey the concept of "esthetic enjoyment"[10] as heightened experience arises from the observation of everyday experience and instrumentally rationalizing why we say and act as we do.

Dewey makes few specific references to historical philosophers in *Art as Experience*.[11] An especially telling indication of Dewey's naturalistic philosophical orientation is the way he draws support from a lengthy passage from Keats that uses analogies similar to Dewey's own between

---

5   John C. Gilmore, "Dewey and Gadamer on the Ontology of Art," *Man and World* 20 (1987): 205.
6   Richard Rorty, *Consequences of Pragmatism* (Minneapolis: University of Minnesota Press, 1982).
7   Jürgen Habermas, *Moral Consciousness and Communicative Action*, trans. C. Lenhardt and S. Weber Nicholsen (Cambridge, MA: MIT Press, 1990).
8   Gilmore, "Dewey and Gadamer on the Ontology of Art," 205.
9   Dewey, *AE*, 5.
10 Dewey's spelling of "aesthetic" as "esthetic" is preserved in all of my subsequent quotations from *AE*.
11 The chapter on "The Challenge to Philosophy" is an exception this regard. Dewey, *AE*, 272–297.

human and animal behaviors to explain how the mind operates. Dewey concludes that reason "must fall back upon imagination—upon the embodiment of ideas in emotionally charged sense." Even the greatest philosopher "exercises an animal-like preference to guide his thinking to its conclusions."[12]

In "The Relevance of the Beautiful," Gadamer makes similar points to demonstrate how reason and imagination support each other, but he founds these observations on a rereading of the thought of previous Continental philosophers such as Kant and Hegel rather than on animalistic analogy. Gadamer's hermeneutic reinterpretation of the ideas of his philosopher forebears allows him to incorporate their concepts into his own original thinking. His discussion of aesthetics draws central illustrations and ideas from both Plato and Aristotle, both Kant and Hegel, seemingly rethinking the entire historical development of philosophy as he goes.

Dewey's anti-foundationalism runs deeper; he seems to set Philosophy aside altogether.[13] Dewey reveals an understanding similar to atheistic existentialism, with its view that there is nothing beyond ourselves and we are therefore determined by our interaction with and adaptation to conditions of our environment. In the absence of divine revelation, the insights of imagination must suffice:

> Ultimately there are but two philosophies. One of them accepts life and experience in all its uncertainty, mystery, doubt, and half-knowledge and turns that experience upon itself to deepen and intensify its own qualities—to imagination and art. This is the philosophy of Shakespeare and Keats.[14]

And, by implication, it is the philosophy accepted by Dewey, in which "turning experience on itself to deepen and intensify its own qualities" seems to suggest a kind of hermeneutic circle. Accepting life "in all its uncertainty," without hope of discovering a founding Truth or having divinely guaranteed morality to fall back on, is the hard lesson of pragmatism. Rorty, citing Sartre's injunction that we must learn to do without God, describes it as the "sense that there is nothing deep down inside us except what we have put there ourselves, no criterion that we have not created in the course of creating a practice, no standard of

---

12 Dewey, *AE*, 33–4.
13 Dewey later issues a caution on the influence that the German convention of capitalizing nouns has had on German thought. *AE*, 252:n.
14 Ibid., 34.

rationality that is not an appeal to such a criterion, no rigorous argumentation that is not obedience to our own conventions."[15]

The Post-Philosophical Debate

In his account of the alignment of pragmatism and hermeneutic philosophy, Jürgen Habermas demonstrates how both reject the ultimate claim to reason that the philosophical thought of Kant and Hegel embraces.

> Pragmatism and hermeneutics oust the traditional notion of the solitary subject that confronts objects and becomes reflective only by turning itself into an object. In its place they put an idea of cognition that is mediated by language and linked to action. Moreover, they emphasize the web of everyday life and communication surrounding "our" cognitive achievements. The latter are intrinsically intersubjective and cooperative. [No matter how] this web is conceptualized, whether as "form of life," "lifeworld," "practice," "linguistically mediated interaction," a "language game," "convention," "cultural background," "tradition," "effective history,"...these commonsensical ideas, though they may function quite differently, attain a status that used to be reserved for the basic concepts of epistemology. Pragmatism and hermeneutics, then, accord a higher position to acting and speaking than to knowing. ...Instead of focusing introspectively on consciousness, these two points of view look outside at objectifications of action and language.[16]

In the sphere of language, Rorty shares Habermas' view that analytic and continental thought are in alignment, having reached a similar conclusion, though by diverse means: "analytic philosophy of language was able to...adopt a naturalistic, behavioristic attitude toward language, [leading] it to the same outcome as the "Continental" reaction against the traditional Kantian problematic [of transcendent experience and consciousness], the reaction found in Nietzsche and Heidegger."[17] Habermas adds that unlike Kantian self-reflection, the action and language of pragmatic and hermeneutic thought "have no justificatory function any more save one: to expose the need for foundational knowledge as unjustified."[18] Rorty argues that both pragmatic and Continental philosophers are telling us that "attempts to get back behind language to something which "grounds" it, or which it "expresses," or to which it might hope to be "adequate," have not worked." This kind of philosophical anti-foundationalism, also applied to the history of philosophy, links the thought of Dewey and Heidegger.[19]

---

15 Rorty, *Consequences of Pragmatism*, xlii.
16 Habermas, *Moral Consciousness and Communicative Action*, 9–10.
17 Rorty, *Consequences of Pragmatism*, xxi.
18 Habermas, *Moral Consciousness and Communicative Action*, 10.
19 Rorty, "Overcoming the Tradition: Heidegger and Dewey," in *Consequences of Pragmatism*, 37–59.

Habermas asserts that pragmatism and hermeneutics have shown that such a foundation is not needed, while Rorty believes that they have given up the search for one because, in spite of repeated efforts and changes of approach over the centuries, such a foundation has not, and indeed cannot, be found.

Rorty writes that the "urge to make philosophy into Philosophy is to make it the search for some final vocabulary, which can somehow be known in advance to be the common core, the truth of, all the other vocabularies which might be advanced in its place. This is the urge which the pragmatist thinks should be repressed, and which a post-Philosophical culture would have succeeded in repressing."[20] Rorty seems to be suggesting that philosophy must give up any claim to rationality and embrace a new role as "edifying conversation." This construct combines features of three types of saying farewell to philosophy, as outlined by Habermas: therapeutic relief (Wittgenstein), heroic overcoming (Heidegger and Bataille), and hermeneutic reawakening (contemporary neo-Aristotelians).[21] Habermas challenges Rorty's position because he is convinced that "even a philosophy that has been taught its limits by pragmatism and hermeneutics will not be able to find a resting place in edifying conversation *outside* the sciences without immediately being drawn back into argumentation, that is, justificatory discourse."[22]

While eschewing the pretensions of Kantian and Hegelian foundational Philosophy as anticipatory cognitive usher and final judge of truth in all intellectual inquiries, Habermas believes against Rorty that philosophy "can and ought to retain its claim to reason" in a more modest, self-critical form as "stand-in...and interpreter,"[23] thus preserving its status as "guardian of rationality."[24] To achieve this, Habermas proposes a "unity of reason" that in fact reunites three aspects of rationality—scientific truth, moral justice, and aesthetic taste—that have been considered since the beginning of modernity following Kant as separate aspects of reason rather than as parts of a whole. The ground for this reunification is none other than our communicative everyday life, our shared lifeworld.[25]

---

20 Rorty, *Consequences of Pragmatism*, xlii.
21 Habermas, *Moral Consciousness and Communicative Action*, 11–14.
22 Ibid., 14; Habermas' emphasis.
23 Ibid., 4.
24 Rorty's term, cited i n ibid., 3.
25 Habermas, "Philosophy as Stand-in and Interpreter," in ibid., 1–20. See Chapter 6 for further discussion of Habermasian unity of reason.

Reunifying Art and Experience

The aesthetics of both Dewey and Gadamer also seek a reunification, one that will recover "the continuity of esthetic experience with normal processes of living." For Dewey, the philosophies of art since Kant emphasize "beyond all reason the merely contemplative character of the esthetic" and offer a record of the development of the chasm between producers and consumers of art.[26] Gadamer, while crediting Kant for being the first to treat the experience of art and beauty as its own philosophical inquiry and as more than a question of subjective taste, sees philosophical thought as the force that *precipitated* the isolation of art from everyday life. According to Gadamer, Kant's "autonomy of the aesthetic" broke ground for art "as art." Kantian "disinterested delight" suggested that we have no practical interest in art: it has no real purpose for us, and therefore we cannot ask what purpose our enjoyment serves.[27]

Dewey and Gadamer agree that it was not until the Enlightenment that the alienation of art from everyday life gained momentum. In contrast, the ancient Greek concept of art was fully integrated with everyday life.[28] Gadamer argues that the very concept of "art" as understood by the ancient Greeks lies outside the philosophical tradition because it belongs to the Aristotelian realm of knowledge "appropriate to production." In both the craftsman's and artist's production, the work becomes separated from the activity of making it. According to Gadamer's reading of Plato, the producer's knowledge and skills are secondary to considerations of use, because someone other than the producer decides what is to be made. "Thus the concept of the work points toward the sphere of common use and common understanding as the realm of intelligible communication."[29] Gadamer retells Plato's story from *Phaedrus* of human souls regaining their wings through the experience of love and the beautiful that give us "lasting remembrance of the true world" to illustrate that "the essence of the beautiful does not lie in some realm simply opposed to reality... The ontological function of the beautiful is to bridge the chasm between the ideal and the real."[30] Dewey locates the sources of the modern arts in rites and celebrations, all "part of the significant life of an organized community," thus explaining how the Greek theory of art as imitation or

---

26   Dewey, *AE*, 10.
27   Gadamer, *RB*, 18–19.
28   See Dewey, *AE*, 7–8, and Gadamer, *RB*, 12–13.
29   Gadamer, *RB*, 12–13.
30   Ibid., 15.

reproduction arose and testifying to the close link of "the fine arts with daily life." He cites Plato's connecting of art to civic institutions as evidence that the ancient Greeks experienced music as "an integral part of the ethos and the institutions of the community."[31]

Both Dewey and Gadamer discuss the subsequent development of modern art that is "divorced from its original context of life" and wishes to be "only" art. Gadamer's account points to Kantian aesthetic autonomy as the source of this development, but he also discusses its anthropological dimension: nineteenth-century artists ceased to live in the community, instead creating their own communities (followings) and claiming their personal artistic message as "the only true one."[32] Dewey attributes this peculiar "esthetic individuation"—marked by modern artists who willfully separate themselves from the normal flow of social services, emphasize self-expression and independence over other values, and create "increasingly esoteric" artistic products—to the conditions in modern society that create "the gulf...between producer and consumer." The separation of art from everyday life has its real roots not in philosophical theory nor in the changing attitudes of artists, but in what Dewey calls the "museum conception of culture," in which carefully-crafted everyday objects from other cultures are separated from their original purposes as signs of "group and clan membership" and treated as art objects in institutions memorializing western imperialism.[33] Dewey would likely agree with Walter Benjamin's observation, also made in the 1930s, of a shift of the social function of art from ritual to politics.[34] Further, Dewey's use of the term "product" to denote how the art work functions in society anticipates the Horkheimer/Adorno thesis of art as a capitalist commodity.[35]

Drawing copiously on examples and analogies from both human society and the natural world, Dewey argues that "the actual work of art is what the product does with and in experience."[36] For Dewey, experience is a process with phases of doing and undergoing, during which meanings accrue. Aesthetic experience is a heightening of everyday experience through emotion. The producer of a work of art must be deeply involved

---

31 Dewey, *AE*, 7–8.
32 Gadamer, *RB*, 6–7.
33 Dewey, *AE*, 6–8.
34 Cf. Walter Benjamin, "The Work of Art in the Age of Its Technological Reproducibility: Second Version," in *The Work of Art in the Age of Its Technological Reproducibility and Other Writings on Media* (Cambridge: Belnap Press, 2008), 25.
35 Cf. Max Horkheimer and Theodor W. Adorno, *Dialectic of Enlightenment*, trans. E. Jephcott (Palo Alto, CA: Stanford University Press, 2002).
36 Dewey, *AE*, 3.

in its production for the result to be properly aesthetic and capable of being perceived as such. He distinguishes between experience and having an experience. Whether dominantly aesthetic or not, the unity of every experience, writes Dewey, "is constituted by a single quality that pervades the entire experience in spite of the variation of its constituent parts." This quality is the aesthetic, and emotion is the force that gives "qualitative unity to materials externally disparate and dissimilar." They operate to bring the experience to its unified conclusion as "the consummation of a movement."[37]

Reinterpreting Kant's constructs of genius, taste, and the free play of the imagination, Gadamer offers "fundamental human experiences" as the anthropological basis of our experience of art. He attempts to show that the "definition of art as the creation of genius can never really be divorced from the con-geniality of the one who experiences it. A kind of free play is at work in both cases." For Gadamer the aesthetic taste of the perceiver involves "a similar play of the imagination and the understanding," allowing concepts to "come to reverberate" (Kant's phrase) like a clavichord "as a kind of sounding board capable of articulating the free play of the imagination."[38] In *Truth and Method* Gadamer investigates the nature of Experience (*Erlebnis*) and notes the

> affinity between the structure of Erlebnis as such and the mode of being of the aesthetic... The work of art is understood as the consummation of the symbolic representation of life, and towards this consummation every experience already tends. Hence it is itself marked out as the object of aesthetic experience. For aesthetics the conclusion follows that so-called Erlebniskunst (art based on experience) is art per se.[39]

For Gadamer, the transforming experience of art occurs when the work of art achieves its hermeneutic identity, and it is in this moment that the meaning of the work is consummated. The meaning of the work is in the very experience of it, which, even in the literary and visual arts, Gadamer seems to conceive of as a type of performance. He asserts that every work of art "leaves the person who responds to it a certain leeway, a space to be filled by himself... We must trace [the form] out as we see it because we must construct it actively—something required by every composition, graphic or musical, in drama or in reading. There is constant cooperative activity here." It is this directed activity of "performing a constant

---

37 Ibid., 37, 42.
38 Gadamer, *RB*, 21.
39 Gadamer, *Truth and Method*, 70.

hermeneutic movement guided by the anticipation of the whole, and finally fulfilled by the individual in the realization of the total sense," that secures the work's hermeneutic identity. In Gadamer's view it is this identity alone that constitutes the meaning of the work.[40]

Dewey refers to aesthetic receptivity as "an act of the going-out of energy in order to receive," comparable in its general outline to the actions of the artist in creating the work.

> With the perceiver, as with the artist, there must be an ordering of the elements of the whole that is in form, although not in details, the same as the process of organization the creator of the work consciously experienced. Without an act of recreation the object is not perceived as a work of art. The artist selected, simplified, clarified, abridged and condensed according to his interest. The beholder must go through these operations according to his point of view and interest. In both, an act of abstraction, that is of extraction of what is significant, takes place. In both, there is comprehension in its literal signification—that is, a gathering together of details and particulars physically scattered into an experienced whole.[41]

The above constitutes an authentic aesthetic experience because the percipient's activity "does not stand by itself but is linked to the activity of which it is the consequence." Conversely, the artist while aesthetically engaged in his work "embodies in himself the attitude of the perceiver."[42]

For both Dewey and Gadamer, continuous movement is the essential marker of the continuity of all experience. Dewey speaks of energies and the rhythm of the live creature's interaction with and adaptation to its environment. His basic rhythm of life is characterized by a back-and-forth movement, between tension (temporary disunity, loss of integration between organism and environment) and balance (recovery of unity, integration; order, form). Tension implies an activity of moving toward moments of balance. Unless there is a state of inertia (stasis), the balance (equilibrium) is always a temporary achievement as the motion continues toward next temporary loss of balance. Inertia characterizes a life of mere subsistence, where the organism does not respond to the temporary lack of "adequate adjustment with surroundings" with some compensating activity aimed at helping to restore balance. A life is enhanced beyond mere subsistence "when a temporary falling out [of balance] is a transition to a more extensive balance of the energies of the organism with those of the conditions under which it lives." For Dewey these biological facts reach to the roots of aesthetic experience: organic adaptation through expansion

---

40   Gadamer, *RB*, 25–28.
41   Dewey, *AE*, 53–54.
42   Ibid., 48–49.

(compensating activity) is the "germ" of "balance and harmony attained through rhythm."[43] Aesthetic experience is thus "heightened vitality...our sole demonstration of a stability that is not stagnation but is rhythmic and developing."[44] In *Truth and Method*, Gadamer writes in a similar vein: "Aesthetic experience is not just one kind of experience among others, but represents the essence of experience per se."[45]

Dewey's concept of experience is one that transforms the interaction of organism and environment into participation and communication.[46] Gadamer also finds the fulfillment of experience in participatory communication. Gadamer conceives it in terms of the goalless back-and-forth movement of the "essential anthropological function" of play.[47] Citing the studies of Huizinga and Guardini on play in religious and cult practices, Gadamer discusses play as "free impulse" that has the source of its movement within itself. The rationality of play is non-purposive because we impose rules and order on the movements of play only as if we have a specific purpose. Because it has no goal, play also has no end, and we achieve identity in repetition. According to Gadamer, what play intends is the activity of playing, thus taking a step in the direction of communication. "If something is represented here—if only the movement of play itself—...the onlooker "intends" it, just as in the act of play I stand over against myself as an onlooker... Play is thus the self-representation of its own movement." The consummation of play as a communicative act needs a "playing along with...an inner sharing in this repetitive movement."[48] Play disregards separation between player and watcher, as the latter also "takes part." Crucial to Gadamer's construct of play are its embedded rational features, which ensure that this is "serious" play. The continuity of the inherent seriousness of play from ritual practices to works of art is supported by the fact that primitive human societies do not distinguish between categories of human activity that could be classed as play and those that could be classed as work, suggesting a cultural understanding that both "playfulness" and "seriousness" are present in play.[49]

---

43 Ibid., 14.
44 Ibid., 19.
45 Gadamer, *Truth and Method*, 70.
46 Dewey, *AE*, 22.
47 See Gadamer's discussions of this theory in the first part of *Truth and Method*, in "The Relevance of the Beautiful," and in "The Play of Art" (*RB*, 123–30).
48 Gadamer, *RB*, 22–24.
49 Thomas M. Malaby, "Anthropology and play: the contours of playful experience" in *New Literary History* 40(1) (2009): 208. See Chapter 5 for further discussion of Gadamer's theory of play.

Gadamer's "playing" and "playing along with" roughly correspond to the doing and undergoing phases in Dewey's conception of aesthetic experience. These phases occur both in alternation and in an essential relationship to each other. "The conception of conscious experience as a perceived relation between doing and undergoing enables us to understand the connection that art as production and perception and appreciation as enjoyment sustain to each other."[50] The undergoing phase brings a unified experience to an active culmination that Dewey likens to the "closure of a circuit of energy." No experience is unified—it does not qualify as "*an experience*"—unless it has aesthetic quality. For that aesthetic quality to emerge, the experience must be emotionally charged.[51] Artistic craftsmanship must be "loving," writes Dewey, "it must care deeply for the subject matter upon which skill is exercised." The artist must have had "an experience of his own that he was concerned to have those share who look at his products. To be truly artistic, a work must also be esthetic—that is, framed for enjoyed receptive perception. Constant observation is, of course, necessary for the maker while he is producing." In Gadamer's terms, the artist must "stand over against" himself "as an onlooker," embodying, as Dewey puts it, "the attitude of the perceiver while he works." But if the artist's perception is not also aesthetic in nature, it is "a colorless and cold recognition of what has been done, used as a stimulus to the next step in a process that is essentially mechanical."[52] It is emotion that both secures and governs the relationship between the doing and undergoing phases of experience. Dewey later calls it the emotional phase: it is the phase that "binds parts together into a single whole."[53]

For Dewey it is emotion that separates perception, seeing "for the sake of seeing what is there," from moments of "mere recognition…when we are momentarily distracted from something else that holds our attention."[54] Recognition is a fleeting "cue for bare identification," a "perception arrested before it has a chance to freely develop" in the consciousness. Perception as a receptive process is

> an act of reconstructive doing, and consciousness becomes fresh and alive. This act of seeing involves the cooperation of motor elements even though they remain implicit and do not become overt, as well as cooperation of all funded ideas that may serve to complete the new picture that is forming. …There [must be] resistance

---

50 Dewey, *AE*, 46–47.
51 Ibid., 41–43.
52 Ibid., 48.
53 Ibid., 55.
54 Ibid., 52, 24.

between new and old to secure consciousness of the experience that is had. ...An act of perception proceeds by waves that extend serially throughout the entire organism.

Perception is not something to which emotion can be added, because the "perceived object or scene is [already] emotionally pervaded throughout."[55]

For Gadamer, this experience-consummating, work-identifying perception is also a process of seeing, of revealing to oneself as percipient what can be seen in the work of art. This process, the performance of a "constant hermeneutic movement...in which we unite and bring together many different aspects," allows us to see what the artist evokes "as it really is."[56] Gadamer defines perception as a taking of the non-differentiated whole "as true," as opposed to merely collecting diverse "sensory impressions." Gadamer uses the phrase "aesthetic non-differentiation" to suggest the "deep structure of perception." In contrast, criticism of an artwork or performance through the selection of individual components of the work or performance would be a kind of "aesthetic differentiation," what Gadamer calls a "secondary procedure [whereby] we abstract from whatever meaningfully addresses us in the work of art and wholly restrict ourselves to a "purely aesthetic" evaluation." Gadamer:

> The artistic experience is constituted precisely by the fact that we do not distinguish between the particular way the work is realized and the identity of the work itself. That is not only true of the performing arts and the mediation or reproduction that they imply. It is always true that **the work as such still speaks to us in an individual way as the same work, even in repeated and different encounters with it**. Where the performing arts are concerned, of course this identity in variation must be realized in a two-fold manner insofar as the reproduction is as much exposed to identity and variation as the original.[57]

He equates aesthetic non-differentiation with Kant's "cooperative play between imagination and understanding"—understanding which is *not* directed toward a concept, but toward building up "the autonomous significance of perception" whereby perception is "no longer simply embedded within the pragmatic contexts of everyday life in which it functions, but expresses and presents itself in its own significance."[58]

---

55   Ibid., 53.
56   Gadamer, *RB*, 28–29.
57   Ibid., 29; my emphasis.
58   Ibid., 28–30.

The Work of Art as Expressive Object and as Symbol

For Dewey, the "work" of art, due to the flexibility of the use of the English noun, can refer to both process—the expressive act—and the resulting product.[59] Again he emphasizes continuity, and rejects the common philosophical oppositions of individual and universal, of subject and object, as having "no place in the work of art. Expression as personal act and as objective result are organically connected with each other." He proposes an alternative to traditional understandings of representation in art: "representation may also mean that **the work of art tells something to those who enjoy it about the nature of their own experience of the world**: that it presents the world in a new experience which they undergo."[60] This seems to have a parallel in what Gadamer, like Heidegger in "The Origin of the Work of Art," calls "an increase in being" offered by the experience of art. Gadamer's concept of the symbolic in art "rests upon an intricate interplay of showing and concealing."[61] According to Gadamer, the "symbolic does not simply point toward a meaning, but rather allows that meaning to present itself. ... The work of art does not simply refer to something, because what it refers to is actually there. We could say that the work of art signifies an increase in being."[62]

Dewey makes a distinction between scientific statement and artistic expression similar to the distinction others make between language and music as modes of communication, or between truth as correctness and aletheia. While science states meanings, art expresses them. A statement lays out conditions in a way that they can serve as directions to arrive at the experience, but it does not provide the experience itself. Art, rather than leading to an experience, *constitutes* the experience, because it "does not operate in the dimension of correct descriptive statement but in that of experience itself."[63] Gadamer frames artistic statements as challenges that must be answered. First, we must be open to being addressed by art, to learn "to listen to what art has to say," and then answer it through actively "playing along." Gadamer:

---

59 Cf. the "working" of the work in Heidegger's "The Origin of the Work of Art." Heidegger refers to how the work "works" in the world rather than to the "work" of creating the work.
60 Dewey, *AE*, 82–83: my emphasis.
61 Gadamer, *RB*, 33.
62 Ibid., 34–35.
63 Dewey, *AE*, 84–85.

> [The work's hermeneutic] identity consists precisely in there being something to "understand," that it asks to be understood in what it "says" or "intends." The work issues a challenge which expects to be met. It requires an answer—an answer that can only be given by someone who accepted the challenge. And that answer must be his own, and given actively. The participant belongs to the play.

Genuine aesthetic experience is available only to one who "plays along… who performs in an active way himself…"[64]

Gadamer argues against contemporary artists who renounce the "unity of the work" as something that pushes audiences away. Because each work of art has a deeply grounded hermeneutic identity, it is *not* "closed off from the person who turns to [the work] or is affected by it. …Even the most fleeting and unique of experiences is intended in its self-identity when it appears or is valued as aesthetic experience."[65] That valuing is expressed in the way that answering a work of art also identifies it as such.

> Any identifiable configuration to which we can apply such expressions as "beautiful," "well-wrought," "eloquent," and so on, has already been identified in its own right as soon as we characterize it in this way… even a mobile enjoys an identity of its own, just as a unique dance, a bravura performance, or an organ improvisation does… Something presents itself here as something upon which we pass judgment. Even if it has only been seen or heard once, it still represents something that has taken shape as a work.[66]

Giving the example of household items exhibited as artworks, Gadamer presupposes that all artistic production is intended "to be what it is." The "determinate character" of such an item is in the effect it produces in aesthetic experience. It may not become a classic, but it is still a "work" according to its hermeneutic identity. Gadamer's remarks on "intended self-identity when it appears or is valued as aesthetic experience"[67] offer a convincing answer to a central question of Arthur C. Danto's aesthetic inquiry in *The Transfiguration of the Commonplace*—how can we distinguish between works of art and "mere real things?"[68]

Dewey singles out art as the only medium of complete community of experience, of "unhindered communication between man and man that can occur in a world full of gulfs and walls that limit community of

---

64 Gadamer, *RB*, 26.
65 Ibid., 25.
66 Ibid., 145.
67 Ibid., 25.
68 Arthur C. Danto, *Transfiguration of the Commonplace: A Philosophy of Art* (Cambridge, MA: Harvard University Press, 1981), 1–32.

experience."⁶⁹ His conception anticipates the concept of festival as formulated by Gadamer in "The Relevance of the Beautiful." As Gadamer explains,

> A festival is an experience of community and represents community in its most perfect form. A festival is meant for everyone. ...Festive celebration... is clearly distinguished by the fact that here we are not primarily separated, but rather are gathered together. ...Celebrating is an art [that]... consists in an experience of community... in which we are gathered together for something, although no one can say exactly for what it is that we have come together. It is no accident that this experience resembles that of art... The celebration of a festival is, in technical terms, an intentional activity. We celebrate inasmuch as we are gathered for something, and this is particularly clear in the case of the experience of art. It is not simply the fact that we are all in the same place, but rather the intention that unites us and prevents us as individuals from falling into private conservations and private, subjective experiences.⁷⁰

The temporal character of the festive celebration that we enact lies in its irreducible unity: it does not dissolve into a series of separate moments. Gadamer distinguishes between calculated time—time that is merely filled, or must be spent—and the "fulfilled" or "autonomous" time of the festival and the work of art. Using naturalistic terminology strongly reminiscent of Dewey, Gadamer relates the organic unity of the work of art to "a living organism" in which "the various parts are not subordinated to any particular external purpose, but simply serve the self-preservation of the organism as a living being." Both work of art and living organism "with its internally structured unity" display "autonomous temporality."⁷¹

Gadamer asks, "why does the understanding of what art is today pose a task for thinking?"⁷² In framing the question, he proceeds from the basic principle that our thought must encompass both the "great traditional art" of the past and modern art, presupposing that both are legitimate art forms and that they "do belong together." For Gadamer the essence of spirit is a Hegelian unity of past and present: "the ability to move within the horizon of an open future and an unrepeatable past" constitutes a "profound continuity" that is often referred to as the Gadamerian "fusion of horizons."⁷³ Dewey speaks of artistic expression as the result of a union between the influence of past events and the immediacy and individuality of the present

---

69 Dewey, *AE*, 105.
70 Gadamer, *RB*, 39–40.
71 Ibid., 43.
72 Ibid., 45.
73 Ibid., 9–10.

occasion.[74] For both Gadamer and Dewey, then, the past is what marks us as members of a community, while the immediacy of the present and the horizon of possibilities it holds before us mark us as individuals. Giving the example of the Athenian Parthenon, Dewey also emphasizes the union of old and new as trans-cultural continuity: "The one who sets out theorize about the esthetic experience embodied in the Parthenon must realize in thought what the people into whose lives it entered had in common, as creators and as those who were satisfied with it, with people in our own homes and on our own streets."[75]

Gadamer's question regarding art as a task for thinking also points to the nature of the aesthetic experience as *thought*. Dewey often refers to aesthetic perception as "esthetic enjoyment," but this emotion-pervaded experience is by no means exclusively emotional. Constant thought takes place throughout in a "rhythm of loss of integration with environment and recovery of union" in which emotion is simply the "conscious sign" of impending discord, creating the human desire for regaining that union with the environment. Dewey explains that the difference between aesthetic and scientific thinking is not a difference in kind, but rather a difference "of tempo and emphasis." The artist relishes moments of tension for their potential for being creatively resolved, while the scientist's interest in problems leads her directly from one resolution to the next problem that has suggested itself from the previous solution.[76] Similarly, the back-and-forth movement of Gadamer's cooperative "play" may be goalless, but it is certainly not mindless: it requires attention, concentration, mental coordination with what is being experienced, and the human capacity for "teaching and learning for ourselves."[77]

As an intellectual activity, this ongoing rhythm can be conceived in Gadamerian terms as the fulfillment of his "task for thinking." This task is demanded by art, which in both Deweyan and Gadamerian aesthetics is not idle material passively waiting to be merely "enjoyed." Rather, the need for interpretation is actively presented by the work of art as an agent that "speaks" to us, telling us something that we must try to understand. For Gadamer the unity of old and new is manifested in the challenge that all art, regardless of when it was created, issues to us. Art requires our intellectual involvement—the movement of serious play or undergoing—

---

74   Dewey, *AE*, 71.
75   Ibid., 4.
76   Ibid., 15.
77   Gadamer, *RB*, 51.

to decipher its meaning, yet it paradoxically keeps that meaning symbolically concealed within itself. The festival brings us together outside of calculated time, within a shared space, and with a sense of common purpose without being sure of what that purpose is—the sharing itself becomes that purpose.

Dewey and Gadamer recognize that unity both in life and art is irreducible. Dewey speaks of "dissolv[ing] the effect of discontinuity" within a culture, not by resolving "one set of events and one of institutions into those which preceded it in time," but by "an expansion of experience that absorbs into itself the values experienced because of life-attitudes, other than those resulting from our own human environment."[78] On the level of the work or art, Gadamer's aesthetic non-differentiation addresses the inseparability of form and content, points up the dangers of trying to abstract discrete moments or components from the whole, and shows us that any attempt to analyze or describe does *only* that, and can never fully explain the experience.

Both Dewey and Gadamer comment on how art shows us the limits of knowledge and understanding, and I would suggest that both can be said to subscribe to Wittgenstein's construct of "irreducible complexity."[79] According to Gadamer, the very existence of the work of art, "its facticity, represents an **insurmountable resistance against any superior presumption that we can make sense of it all.**"[80] Ultimately, as Gadamer periodically states, there are certain questions that "we cannot ask." This is a matter of both unknowability and inexpressibility. We simply do not have adequate means to formulate the answers, and recognizing what language does also means recognizing the limitations of that language. As Dewey writes, "If all meanings could be adequately expressed by words, the arts of painting and music would not exist. There are values and meanings that can be expressed only by immediately visible and audible qualities, and **to ask what they mean** in the sense of something that can be put into words **is to deny their distinctive existence.**"[81] In its seemingly limitless possibilities, art sidesteps language as pragmatics and hermeneutics sidestep Philosophy, making manifest the limits of our understanding and of our potential to understand.

---

78 Dewey, *AE*, 336.
79 Ludwig Wittgenstein, *Philosophical Investigations*, trans. G. E. M. Anscombe (New York: Macmillan, 1958).
80 Gadamer, *RB*, 34; my emphasis.
81 Dewey, *AE*, 74; my emphasis.

If we are adept at listening to what it is telling us, art is capable of simultaneously showing us what we might *already* know due to our accumulated "community of experience" (Dewey's phrase), what we *might* be able to know through thinking and imagination, and what might *never* be known. The very openness of art to possibility reveals that which may always be concealed from us. Thus art has the potential to act as a powerful critique of Philosophy in both the continental and analytical traditions.

Part II

Orphic Intersubjectivity

Chapter 3

The Performer as Co-Composer: "Hearing As" and the Creative Orphic "I"

Through ever-new interpretations, the Orpheus myth has become an enduring source of artistic inspiration and a means of understanding the creative process. The figure of Orpheus is an archetype of the modern creative artist, and the proliferation of permutations of this archetype over time confirms its timeless validity. Paul Ricoeur's language-based model of imagination suggests an approach that treats the Orpheus myth as allegory—extended metaphor—and allows for interpretations of the many ways that Orpheus is "seen as" that yield new meaning and carry forward artistic projects by reference to the old.

With the aid of the writings of Plato and Aristotle, I first discuss aspects of art and imagination as they were understood at the time that Orpheus emerged in classical Greek mythology, relating these to the Orpheus myth itself. After tracing the evolution and accumulation of its interpreted meanings, I look at this myth as projected metaphorical narrative in twentieth-century thought, considering interpretations by Rilke, Blanchot, and Jung. I then consider how Orphic features permeate the modern conception of what it means to be a "composer" and "performer," and attempt to demonstrate that these now-separate concepts are still firmly embedded in the ancient Greek poet-musician duality embodied by Orpheus.

Because the implications of the Orpheus myth are as valid for musical creativity as they are for other spheres of artistic endeavor, I extend Ricoeurian "seeing as" to "hearing as." Applying Husserl's concept of intersubjectivity as understood by Ricoeur, I speculate on the significance of Orpheus for the Bulgarian composer Lazar Nikolov and introduce what I believe is a new interpretation of the Orpheus myth, as a way of understanding the modern relationship between composer and performer and as a model for their creative collaboration. My interpretation, which I term **Orphic intersubjectivity**—the Orphic "I"—was first suggested to me by specificities of Nikolov's series of late compositions known under the collective title *From the Music of Orpheus*.

As a myth about an inspired poet-musician, the Orpheus story is rooted in language and, like all myths, lends itself to metaphorical interpretation. Myths can be perceived "as carriers of the human attempt to attach meaning, or a deeper sense, to our existence. ...*mythos* means narration, and narration is, and has been for all times, a combination of words."[1] The second part of Gérard Bucher's essay "The Orphic Humanity" in *L'imagination de l'origine* takes as its point of departure Heidegger's statement that "all thought that unfolds meaning is poetry, and all poetry is thought."[2] Following Heidegger, Bucher sees the construction of "being-in-the-language" as the communicative calling of poetry, and metaphor as poetry's basic resource. Zupancic points out that the very etymology of the Greek *meta-phorein* suggests that "words lead us into "other" worlds."[3] Metaphor is also at the heart of Ricoeur's language-based hermeneutic theory of imagination, in which the consciousness uses semantic innovation to move beyond the static recognition of seemingly incompatible terms. The cognitive act of apprehending "identity in difference" transforms "saying as" (a manifestation of the regressive imagining of what *already* exists) into "seeing as" (progressive imagining of what *can* exist), allowing a Kantian synthesis to take place and leading to new meaning.[4]

For Heidegger, "all art is in essence poetry." He gives language, which through naming "first brings beings to word and to appearance," a broader conceptual base at the origin of the work of art and treats poetry as "projective saying...which, in preparing the sayable, simultaneously brings the unsayable as such into the world." This allows him to trace all of the separate arts, including music, "back to poesy."[5] In ancient Greece both poetry and music were grouped together in the sphere of inspiration and thought of according to their common means of production: both were

---

1 Metka Zupancic, "In the Beginning was the Word: Reflections on Gérard Bucher's *L'imagination de l'origine*," in *Death, Language, Thought: On Gérard Bucher's L'imagination de l'origine*, ed. M. Zupancic (Summa Publications, 2005), 52.
2 Martin Heidegger, "The Origin of the Work of Art," quoted in Zupancic, ibid., 55.
3 Zupancic, "In the Beginning was the Word," 55.
4 Paul Ricoeur, "Imagination in discourse and action," in *Rethinking Imagination: Culture and Creativity*, ed. G. Robinson and J. Rundell (London: Routledge, 1994), 121-123.
5 Martin Heidegger, "The Origin of the Work of Art," in *Poetry, Language, Thought*, trans. A. Hofstadter (New York: Harper and Row, 1971), 70-1.

sung.⁶ Thus Orpheus is the apparent prototype of Heidegger's "singing poet."

Orpheus, Inspired Poet-Musician of Antiquity

Aristotle distinguishes between poetry's expressed subject matter (resulting from divine inspiration) and the craft of versification that served a merely formal function and could be applied to writings on any subject.[7] Plato uses similar categories in separating "manic" or "frenzied" poetry, where the muses come to the poet and inspire him with "divine madness," from the less-valued "artisan poetry," where the "sane" poet "comes to the door of the Muses, confident that he will be a good poet by art [i.e., mimetic craftsmanship], [but] meets with no success."[8] The inspired, muse-possessed poet appears alongside the philosopher near the top of Plato's hierarchy of human occupations and is referred to as *mousikos*, a word that can be rendered in English as "poet-musician."[9] This modern term is further justified by the fact that Plato applies the word *poiesis* (roughly synonymous with creativity) only to the division of verse and tones in his classification of the arts.[10]

Plato sets the poetry-music pairing apart from other arts (such as sculpture and architecture) because to the ancient Greek understanding, art denotes something crafted in a skillful—*artful*—way in imitation of things that already existed. While still capable of yielding knowledge, the creations of imitative art are interpreted as being illusory, unreal productions. Plato places imitative poetry in this lower category together with the plastic arts in his "purely human" sphere of action, where they simply reproduce the actuality of the world of sense. As the only truly creative art, inspired poetry-music is "regarded as an inordinately higher activity." To Plato it is not an art at all—it is *artless* in the sense that its human manifestations come into being as received spiritual visions and revealed knowledge of ideal existence and absolute being.[11] Heidegger emphasizes this distinction, contrasting what he calls the "two modes of bringing

---

6   Władysław Tatarkiewicz, "Art and Poetry: A Contribution to the History of Ancient Aesthetics," *Studia Logica* (Journal of the Institute of Philosophy and Sociology of the Polish Academy of Sciences, ca. 1940): 383–4.
7   Tatarkiewicz, "Art and Poetry," 382–3.
8   Plato, *Phaedrus*: 245A, quoted in Tatarkiewicz, "Art and Poetry," 397.
9   See for example Robert McGahey, *The Orphic Moment: Shaman to Poet-Thinker in Plato, Nietzsche, and Mallarme* (Albany: State University of New York Press, 1994).
10   Tatarkiewicz, "Art and Poetry," 400.
11   Tatarkiewicz, "Art and Poetry," 395–400.

forth...knowledge as experienced in the Greek manner": the educated craftsmanship of making and the "bringing forth of present beings."[12]

Operating in the higher "semi-divine" Platonic sphere of action, the inspired poet-musician is "a man of the gods" through whom oracles from the heavens are made known to men. Throughout *Ion* Plato refers specifically to how he imagines this mediating function of the poet-musician to work:

> The Muse inspires men herself and then by means of these inspired persons the inspiration spreads to others... For all the good epic poets utter all these fine poems not from art but as inspired and possessed... The poet is unable ever to [create] until he has been inspired and put out of his senses, and his mind is no longer in him... For not by art do they utter these things, but by divine influence... It is God himself who speaks and addresses us through them... Those fine poems are not human or the work of men, but divine and the work of gods, and the poets are merely the interpreters of gods.[13]

Later the Neoplatonic philosophers discuss the workings of inspiration in the imagination. According to Iamblichus the poet-musician becomes a passive conveyor of "divine visions [that] occupy [his] imaginative faculty...driven by the will of the gods."[14] As Emma Clarke observes, in Neoplatonic thinking, "an inspired individual is not thinking or using his imagination—his imagination...is manipulated by the gods and receives divine *phantasmata* during inspiration."[15] It becomes clear that the consciousness of the poet-musician is thought to have been acted upon from the outside, and his works are then the expression of *re*ceived rather than internally *con*ceived knowledge. As this knowledge "makes itself known" to the poet-musician, it is immediately revealed to those who hear his performance.

This idea of found knowledge is embedded in each of the two complementary Greek myths explaining the origin of music. In the version associated with the cult of Apollo, Apollo's brother Hermes discovers the potential of a tortoise shell to resonate and invents the *lyre*, a plucked string instrument related to the modern harp. Here music is an ordering of sound as it is found in the actual world. In the version associated with the cult of Dionysos, music originates as the human reaction to an emotional shock:

---

12 Heidegger, "The Origin of the Work of Art," 57.
13 Plato, *Ion*: 533–34, trans. W. Lamb, quoted in Tatarkiewicz, "Art and Poetry," 398.
14 Iamblichus, *De Mysteriis*, quoted in Algis Uzdavinys, *Orpheus and the Roots of Platonism* (London: The Matheson Trust, 2011), 25.
15 Emma C. Clarke, *Iamblichus' De Mysteriis: A Manifesto of the Miraculous* (Ashershot: Ashgate, 2001), 84–85, quoted in Uzdavinys, *Orpheus and the Roots of Platonism*, 25.

the screams of Medusa's sisters following Medusa's beheading. Here the sound comes from within, but it is triggered by something external to the person who produces it. Athena is so moved that she invents the *aulos*, a wind instrument related to the modern oboe.[16] These two interpretations of the nature of music roughly correspond to the mimetic (imitative) and cathartic (powerfully emotional) theories of human production propagated by ancient Greek thinkers.[17] The Apollonian and Dionysian principles have been metaphorically related to the rational and the intuitive modes of thinking and being, to form and content, and to the Classical and Romantic principles in music.

A semi-divine mediator between gods and men, the inspired poet-musician is a conduit of privileged knowledge that attained the spiritual world. As such he fulfills the function of poetry as prophecy: more than telling, the narrative of poetry was a *fore*telling. In his ability to inspire others the poet-musician acts as a shaman, with seemingly magical powers of persuasion. His persuasive power links him to rhetorical orators and is considered either a praiseworthy "superhuman" trait, or one that is dangerously irrational.[18] Fulfilling these important functions is a matter of being chosen, in which individual will does not play a role. A "shamanist contradiction" arises from the conflict between the poet-musician's sense of personal freedom and his actual social status as a mere spokesman for higher powers.[19] This conflict is summed up succinctly in the *Odyssey* of Homer, whose poet-musician Phemios says, "I am self-taught. The gods have implanted into my heart songs of all kinds."[20]

This mediation between gods and men is fully in evidence in the case of Orpheus. An accepted scholarly view is that Orpheus "is an eponymous Thracian shaman who mediates Mycenaean-West Asian religion and northern shamanism (viz. Dionysos and Apollo)."[21] Within himself Orpheus combines the two opposing or balancing roles of religious reformer

---

16 R. Murray Schafer, *The Soundscape: Our Sonic Environment and the Tuning of the World* (Rochester, VT: Destiny Books, 1977), 6.
17 Tatarkiewicz, "Art and Poetry," 394–5.
18 Ibid., 380.
19 Jack Lindsay, *The Clashing Rocks* (London: Chapman and Hall, 1965), 317, cited in Robert McGahey, *The Orphic Moment: Shaman to Poet-Thinker in Plato, Nietzsche, and Mallarme* (Albany: State University of New York Press, 1994), 8.
20 Homer, *Odyssey*, book 22, quoted in Lindsay, *The Clashing Rocks*, 347, and McGahey, *The Orphic Moment*, 8.
21 See Lindsay, *The Clashing Rocks*; E. R. Dodds, *The Greeks and the Irrational* (Berkeley and Los Angeles: University of California Press, 1951); Mircea Eliade, *Zalmoxis* (Chicago: University of Chicago Press, 1972); cited in McGahey, *The Orphic Moment*, 7.

and poet-musician. As Robert McGahey explains, the medium of mediation between these two roles is "the common element of incantation (*epoidos*). The term is related to the archaic Odyssean word *oima*, designating "song as way" [and] linking the older tribal shaman with the lyric and dramatic poet of the classical era." A similar dualism between old and new is found in Orphism, which is both a reformation of existing religious practice and a return to earlier religious practice.[22] Just such meetings of new and old are crucial to the hermeneutics of Ricoeur's imagination theory, revealing another aspect of its potential for disclosing emerging meanings through the metaphoric juxtaposition of semantic innovation.

In the fifth century B.C. Orpheus emerges as mediator or "hybrid figure between Apollo and Dionysos," combining features of Apollo as Olympian principle with features of Dionysos as chthonian principle and thereby reconciling or absorbing the differences between the established cult of the god Apollo and the younger, competing cult of the half-god Dionysos.[23] In his enumeration of ten mythemes of the Orpheus myth, McGahey convincingly shows how the myth's Apollonian and Dionysian strands become ever more tightly interwoven. The "enactment of a concerto" is his musical metaphor for the manner of Orpheus' death and its representation in sound: "the solo voice, accompanied by the [Apollonian] *lyre*…against the concerted performance of the Maenads: shrieking, drumming, sometimes wailing on the [Dionysian] *aulos*."[24]

The internal tension between Orpheus as inspired, senseless mouthpiece of the gods and his sense of himself as a free individual—the "shamanist contradiction" mentioned above—is resolved first in his looking back, then in his "death concerto." The Apollonian solo voice delineates Orpheus as an individual, manifesting Nietzsche's *principium individuationis* against a "primal chthonic ground," the mysterious primordial unity of Nietzsche's *Ur-Eine*.[25] It allows him to emerge transformed—
as a new version of himself—through a metaphoric recombination of Apollonian and Dionysian elements contained within him. In Ricoeurian terms, the possibility of song remains, but these allegorical events allow us to "see" song in new ways—as the possibility and process of individuation (a rethinking of why we sing), and as a projection into the future that

---

22 McGahey, *The Orphic Moment*, 8–9.
23 Ibid., 11.
24 Ibid., 18.
25 Ibid., 19.

continues as Orpheus' dismembered head, floating down the river Hebrus, continues to sing. In the Orpheus myth, song itself emerges as the ultimate mediating force.

Ricoeurian Implications of the Orpheus Myth

From the earliest sources of the Orpheus myth through its many subsequent transpositions in literature and art, Orpheus

> represents the old and new at once. Thus he becomes a major figure in the era of Hellenistic syncretism as the reputed author of the so-called Orphic theogonies, as a latter-day Moses and as the Greek incarnation of Hermes Trismegistus. In the Christian era he becomes the pacific shepherd, a type or double for Christ. In the Renaissance he is the magus, both the model operator of Ficino's "natural magic" and the principal figure (along with Eurydice) in the spectacular rise of opera... He and Eurydice reappear as figures of the love-death in the Romantic era, after which they undergo a continual development into the modern era, as the themes of love, death, and night are replaced by the act of creation/sacrifice by the Orphic poet out of the void...[26]

To be seen in new ways, Orpheus must first be *said* in new ways. Each of these retellings of the Orpheus myth adds a new layer of narrative and is oriented towards the specific requirements of each new narrator as he relates to his audience and time. But this is a special kind of seeing, because, as Ricoeur states, "the paradox of fiction is that striking out perception is the condition for heightening our vision of things." In Ricoeurian thought, Orpheus corresponds to the icon, the "graphic figure which recreates reality at a higher level of realism," demonstrating that "all symbols—in art and in literature—have the same referential claim to 'remake reality,'" suggesting through imagination new possibilities for action.[27]

The origins of many widely held attitudes about the artist as a social type can be traced to the Orpheus myth. The artist is often seen as alienated, self-centered, morally compromised, reliant on some outside source of inspiration (whether divine or demonic), and controversially influential. But she is also a seer—a visionary with a personal voice, able to look beyond what is visible to the rest of us and to present a new vision in a compelling way, and therefore uniquely positioned to speak for society as a whole. The Orpheus myth offers insights into how we have been historically conditioned to understand what it means to be an artist—in both its positive and negative aspects—and the artist's relationship to society,

---

26 Ibid., 9–10.
27 Paul Ricoeur, "Imagination in discourse and action," 124.

nature, and herself. Among these aspects are the following, which I have arbitrarily selected for enumeration here:

Orpheus as alienated other. He is
- associated with Thrace, i.e., he is not Greek, but "foreign";[28]
- "out of place" among the dead in the underworld because he is still alive;
- cast out of the underworld;
- unwilling to interact socially following his underworld experience, but it brings him closer to nature;[29]
- a prototype of the "exiled soul" as a mythic figure.

Orpheus as non-conformist individual. He
- follows own impulse in looking back at Eurydice;
- not only does not follow established order in looking back, but also creates his own order;[30]
- sings "his own song," even during and after his dismemberment;
- is the symbol of the "primary narcissism" of Herbert Marcuse's "Great Refusal."[31]

Orpheus as morally compromised and emotionally unstable. He
- uses his song subversively, to gain entrance to underworld;
- is under the delusion that he can control his impulses and be "entirely good";[32]
- does not stop himself from going to underworld due to his overwhelming love;
- rejects women but, according to Ovid's version, becomes homosexual;[33]
- receives images and thoughts he can't explain.[34]

---

28 McGahey, *The Orphic Moment*, 7.
29 Ovid, *Metamorphoses*, trans. A. Melville (London: Oxford University Press, 2009), X.
30 Maurice Blanchot, "The Gaze of Orpheus," in *The Gaze of Orpheus and Other Literary Essays*, trans. L. Davis (Barrytown: Station Hill Press, 1981), 99–104.
31 Michael Ure, *Nietzsche's Therapy: Self-cultivation in the Middle Works* (Lanham: Lexington Books, 2008), 244.
32 Carl Gustav Jung, *Visions: Notes of the Seminar Given in 1930–1934*, Vol. 1, ed. C. Douglas (Princeton: Princeton University Press, 1997), 1293.
33 Ovid, *Metamorphoses*, X.
34 Cf. Jean-Paul Sartre's pathologies of imagination in Richard Kearney, *Poetics of Imagining: Modern to Post-modern* (Edinburgh: Edinburgh University Press, 1998), 69–74.

Orpheus as dependent on a "dark force." He needs the underworld experience
- as a catalyst for song-enacted catharsis following an emotional shock.
- where the night and the "fullness of Eurydice's death" serve as his creative inspiration;
- as a venturing into the unknown that opens up a path to artistic creation;
- to realize his transformation through transgression;
- to fulfill his motivating desire to possess.[35]

Orpheus as visionary. He
- is like the traditionally blind bard who "sees" in metaphorical ways;
- sees beyond the second loss of Eurydice;
- sings despite opposing social forces—the Macean women—that are ready to destroy him;
- sings beyond his own physical death;
- sings as both narrative and prophecy;
- sings as both self-expression and universal expression;
- can imagine what does not already exist: his seeing beyond can be likened to projective imagination in the Ricoeurian sense;
- mediates new modes of being.[36]

It has been asserted that "for Rilke and Cocteau and many lesser writers, Orpheus has been a figure for themselves as artists."[37] This kind of identification with Orpheus is a reflection of an underlying dichotomy between the power to create and the ability to speak—what Walter Strauss refers to as "the possibility of song" that modern Orphic voices recognize.[38] "With words comes Orpheus," writes Elizabeth Sewell, whose research into the Orphic tradition led her to develop the Orphic "song as power" paradigm.[39] By personalizing the Orphic universal, it is possible

---

35 For this and the previous three points I am indebted to Maurice Blanchot, "The Gaze of Orpheus."
36 Rainer Maria Rilke, *Ahead of All Parting: The Selected Poetry and Prose of Rainer Maria Rilke*, ed. and trans. S. Mitchell (New York: The Modern Library, 1995).
37 M. Owen Lee, *Virgil as Orpheus: A Study of the Georgics* (New York: SUNY Press, 1996), xii.
38 Walter A. Strauss, *Descent and Return: The Orphic Theme in Modern Literature* (Cambridge: Harvard University Press, 1971), 249.
39 Elizabeth Sewell, *The Orphic Voice: Poetry and Natural History* (New Haven: Yale University Press, 1960), 9.

to wed the intentionality of the creative act to the sense of "bringing forth" as if from a force outside or beyond one's own consciousness. In the case of Rainer Maria Rilke's *Sonnets to Orpheus*, the author writes that "these strange Sonnets...appeared, often many in one day (the first part of the book was written in about three days), completely unexpectedly... I could do nothing but submit, purely and obediently, to the dictation of this inner impulse..."[40]

Focusing on the moment that Orpheus looks back toward Eurydice and loses her forever, Maurice Blanchot finds in it a metaphor for creative inspiration. In Blanchot's essay, "The Gaze of Orpheus," Orpheus' journey to the underworld becomes an allegory for the creative process. Orpheus does not lose Eurydice in looking back because he has already lost her—she is already dead. What he must give up in the moment of looking back is his need to control the process:

> The act of writing begins with Orpheus' gaze, and that gaze is the impulse of desire which shatters the song's destiny and concern, and in that inspired and unconcerned decision reaches the origin, consecrates the song. But Orpheus already needed the power of art in order to descend to that instant. This means: one can only write if one arrives at the instant towards which one can only move through space opened up by the movement of writing. In order to write, one must already be writing. The essence of writing, the difficulty of experience and the leap of inspiration also lie within this contradiction.[41]

For Carl Jung, the moment of looking back is when the "imagination snaps." In Jung's interpretation there is also a release of control, but what is given up is the illusion of an Orpheus-like power over nature, where nature is a metaphor for one's own unconscious. Looking back becomes a symbol of self-acceptance, of coming to terms with our human imperfection:

> Orpheus symbolizes the faculty of man to charm his unconscious powers; he made such sweet music that all the wild animals became tame and gathered round him. That means that we ourselves are capable of making such sweet music that we can gather all our wild animals round us, we can charm all our instincts and impulses. ...but it is black magic in a way: you can only do it when you have enough imagination to deceive yourself into thinking that you are wholly good. ... We can imagine it for a certain length of time, until something black occurs, and then the imagination snaps and up come all the devils. That is the reason why Orpheus was dismembered by the maenads, and Zagreus by the Titans. It shows a certain superior attitude of man, which, aided by his imagination, for a while makes him believe that he can

---

40   Rilke to Countess Margot Sizzo-Noris-Crouy, April 12, 1923, in *Ahead of All Parting*, 575–6.
41   Blanchot, "The Gaze of Orpheus," 104.

walk upon the water; and he really can, the power of the imagination is very great indeed. But mankind invented these myths, and I am quite sure that the whole of Greek mythology was once tribal knowledge..."[42]

Both Blanchot and Jung see Orpheus' looking back as a moment of self-realization. Their perspectives reveal that within the possibility of song lies the opposing possibility of not being able to sing, of losing the power to create. Behind Blanchot's "inspired and unconcerned decision" and Jung's "snap of the imagination" hide fears of not finding inspiration, of losing one's Orphic voice, of failing to invoke that voice at will. Among the twentieth-century writers who dwell on these fears are Samuel Beckett and Franz Kafka, "whose comic Orphic heroes make an ironic descent into Hades convinced of the impossibility of art and the inevitability of silence. Beckett's Orphic mouthpiece in the underworld demonstrates by her compulsive inchoate babble the heroism of the artist who must fail in his or her expressive vocation."[43]

Lazar Nikolov, A Modern-Day Orpheus

In the realm of music, Orpheus can be seen as the prototype for the composer who doubles as the performer of his own compositions. Because he was divinely inspired, Orpheus unified creation and performance in the same spontaneous act. This act can be likened to musical improvisation, which allows for the immediate realization of musical ideas in sound. By expressing himself in sound, a musician interprets existing musical materials.

The origins of the concept of interpretation are traceable to the Greek word *hermeneuein* (to interpret) and to the god Hermes, who is said to have discovered language and writing, "the tools human understanding employs to grasp meaning and to communicate it to others."[44] The wing-footed Hermes carried messages down from the gods, and made them intelligible to humans. As an interpreter of divine thoughts, "he not only bridged physical distances and the ontological gap between divine and human being, [but also] bridged the difference between the visible and the invisible, and between dreams and waking, between the unconscious and

---

42 Carl Gustav Jung, *Visions: Notes of the Seminar Given in 1930–1934,* Vol. 1, ed. C. Douglas (Princeton: Princeton University Press, 1997), 1293.
43 Katherine Kelly, "The Orphic mouth in 'Not I'," in *The Beckett Studies Reader,* ed. S. Gontarski (Gainesville: University Press of Florida, 1993), 127.
44 Jane O'Dea, *Virtue or Virtuosity? Explorations in the Ethics of Musical Performance* (Westport and London: Greenwood Press, 2000), 2.

the conscious. He is the quicksilver god of sudden insights, ideas, inspirations."[45] Significantly, it was Hermes who invented the lyre, the instrument capable of "translating" the order of the natural world into sounds humans could understand. Orpheus, son of Hermes' brother Apollo, was the lyre-player par excellence, and like Hermes, he was a mediator between gods and men.

Historically, many subsequent composer-performers have "ordered outer sound" through improvisation on their performance instrument—for J. S. Bach, Mozart, Beethoven, and many others, a keyboard instrument—letting musical ideas come to them *as if* from outside their own consciousness. This "as if" has been a key to a creative process that begins intuitively (Dionysos) but relies on existing materials and forms (Apollo). The uniqueness of the resulting composition depends on the particular balance between new or intuited elements and old or found materials. This helps explain later equations of "sounding" with "being sounded," such as Shelley's early nineteenth-century evocation of the composer as an Aeolian harp, paraphrased as follows: "a mouth of Nature, passive yet sensitive, a lonely instrument hung in the forest with its strings stirred by the passing wind."[46]

This improvised sounding out of ideas usually precedes the writing down of a musical composition, thereby rendering it in a more fixed, communicable form. "Notation, the writing out of compositions," writes pianist-composer Ferruccio Busoni, "is primarily an ingenious expedient for catching an inspiration, with the purpose of exploiting it later."[47] Following Hegelian philosophical thought, Theodor W. Adorno's observations on Beethoven also offer insights into the place of notation in the creative process:

> The written form clearly betrays an aversion to a process which does not itself from part of the musical imagination (so that in Beethoven the visual appearance of the notation has little influence on the composition, unlike the case with many, especially modern, composers). In this context, one should think first of the primacy of the whole over the individual part in Beethoven. In the written image the 'idea' or 'inspiration,' the clearly defined individual melody, recedes into the flow of the whole. But something deeper is also involved: the image of the *objectivity* of music,

---

45 Richard E. Palmer, "Hermeneutics and the Disciplines: The Relevance of Gadamer's Philosophical Hermeneutics to Thirty-Six Topics or Fields of Human Activity," lecture delivered at the Department of Philosophy, Southern Illinois University (1999), 2.
46 Louis Rowell, *Thinking About Music* (Amherst: University of Massachusetts Press, 1985), 121.
47 Ferruccio Busoni, *Sketch of a New Esthetic of Music*, trans. T. Baker (New York: G. Schirmer, 1911), 15.

which Beethoven conceived as something existing in itself, not originally made by him... He is the stenographer of the objectified composition, which is something detached from the arbitrariness of individuation. In Benjamin's phrase: 'the clerk recording his own inner life.' What [Beethoven's] handwriting reveals is, really, the shame of the accidental subject before a truth which has been granted him as a whole.[48]

Music manifests the modern Orphic "power as potential impotence" paradox: it is an "incredibly powerful force," yet it is also "infinitely perishable, intangible, and forever in danger of being lost."[49] Like the quicksilver of Hermes, music reveals itself to the senses in so fleeting a manner that its "real existence is in the imagination and the memory."[50] The written notation of music ostensibly resolves this issue by giving it a seemingly permanent expression, but notation is also a compromise in at least three respects. First, "in the transcription of an abstract idea...the idea loses its original form."[51] Second, the musical score is only a representation, "a static, visual and silent entity."[52] Third, the written preservation of music admits the possibility of interpreting someone else's music, of separating the functions of composer and performer. While the ability to improvise remained a core value for musicians, from the nineteenth century on the "demands for technical accomplishment meant that many composers could no longer play their [own] music acceptably, and the rigorous process of acquiring a virtuoso technique made it difficult for a performer to maintain a total commitment to composition."[53]

The Bulgarian composer Lazar Nikolov (1922–2005) started his creative life in the dual Orphic roles of composer and performer: as a performing pianist, he realized his own compositions in sound, as did his teachers Dimiter Nenov and Pancho Vladigerov. By Nikolov's own account, he allowed intuition to lead him in the creative process, and he seems to have regularly engaged in the improvised sounding out of ideas at the piano. But he did not limit his creative impulses to works for this instrument, and after the 1950s he gave up his Orphic composer-performer identity altogether, from that point entrusting the performance of his music—even for piano—to other musicians. While always maintaining that his music "does not express anything specific," much later in his creative

---

48 Teodor W. Adorno, *Beethoven: The Philosophy of Music* (Palo Alto: Stanford University Press, 2002), 9.
49 Rowell, *Thinking About Music*, 73.
50 Ibid., 74.
51 Busoni, *Sketch of a New Esthetic of Music*, 17.
52 O'Dea, *Virtue or Virtuosity?*, 2.
53 Rowell, *Thinking About Music*, 121.

life Nikolov composed a series of pieces with the evocative title *From the Music of Orpheus*.[54] His choice of title was a "specific" reference to "some personal notion, that seemed to connect the sound of Orpheus' music with the sound of the marimba," the instrument he chose for the first piece of his *Orpheus* series.[55] This was the first and only time Nikolov used the marimba in a solo context. The second piece in the series was also for a solo instrument, the viola, and was the first and only Nikolov composition to feature an unaccompanied string instrument.

In contrast to the marimba, an instrument similar to Orpheus' lyre in that it is possible to sound multiple tones simultaneously to produce chords and polyphonic textures, the viola is a melodic instrument, with limited chord-producing capability. The choice of the viola was determined by Valentin Gerov, the musician who had asked Nikolov to compose the piece. It is significant that Nikolov, whose compositional style had always been polyphonic, had consistently insisted that he was not capable of composing a solo work for a melodic instrument without including piano (a chord-producing polyphonic instrument) in the instrumentation. The invocation of Orpheus seems to have unblocked a creative barrier for Nikolov, giving him inspiration and the sense of being able to compose a work of a type that he had never previously attempted.

But for Lazar Nikolov the idea of Orpheus is more than simply "hearing" an imagined ancient music. Orpheus to Nikolov is the performer who "plays in the way that I imagine!"[56] In his double role of composer-performer, Orpheus can be interpreted as a symbol of the performer as co-composer, as the prototype of the contemporary Bulgarian musicians from whom Nikolov expected—and received, by his own account—co-

---

54   In the original Bulgarian, *Iz muzikata na Orfei*. There are three pieces in the series: *From the Music of Orpheus I* for marimba solo (1999?); *From the Music of Orpheus II*—two versions, for viola solo (2001) and for violoncello solo (2002, transcribed by Geoffrey Dean); and *From the Music of Orpheus III* for choir (2002). I had the honor of collaborating with Lazar Nikolov on a recording of his Concertino for cello and orchestra (with conductor Georgi Dimitrov and the Plovdiv Philharmonic) and in the world premiere of his Trio for cello, doublebass, and piano (with Maria Shirokoliyska and Dragomir Yossifov).

55   Lazar Nikolov, program note for his *From the Music of Orpheus I*. Percussionist Tatiana Koleva gave its world premiere on the November 14 concert of the 2000 American Music Week in Bulgaria Festival in Sofia.

56   Lazar Nikolov quoted in Angelina Petrova, *The Composer Lazar Nikolov* (*Kompozitorut Lazar Nikolov*) (Sofia: Bulgarian Academy of Sciences, 2003), 271; my translation.

compositional collaboration in the performance of his music.[57] Nikolov's exposure as a listener to the improvisational skills of the violist Valentin Gerov suggest that in Gerov he recognized another, contemporary variation on the Orphic composer/performer creative duality.

Creative Orphic Intersubjectivity

The concept of co-composition or co-authorship presupposes that the composer has a deep trust in the abilities of his performer, abilities like those of the composer himself. Nikolov recognized and publicly lauded the "creative talent and creative imagination" of the performers with whom he collaborated in new compositions, openly sharing his view that it is possible for the performer to know his composition better than he himself, that "during the performance it becomes the composition of the performer," who transforms the score into "living music."[58] Nikolov implies a kind of identification with his performers in pointing out that "after all, the birthplace of Orpheus is here [in Bulgaria]."[59]

This sense of identification between composer and his performer is a manifestation of what I call **creative Orphic intersubjectivity.** An extension into human action of the semantic innovation of Ricoeur's metaphorical imagination, creative Orphic intersubjectivity is an example of "identity-in-difference" where, in the words of Hegel, "my identity, or *what* I am, is also reflected, and thus revealed to me, by others."[60] Self-consciousness emerges as the product of our consciousness of others, as Orpheus is transformed—revealed to himself—by looking at Eurydice. By extending the "grammatical projection of imaginative variations on the [Kantian] theme 'I can'" to Husserl's theory of intersubjectivity, Ricoeur derives a higher order principle of analogy, demonstrating that "history is

---

57 Lazar Nikolov in an interview with Margarita Kevorkian, "My Life is Creativity" ("Zhivotut mi e tvorchestvo"), in Lazar Nikolov, *My World* (*Moyat svyat*; Sofia: Izdatelstvo "Litse," 1998),120; my translation.
58 Lazar Nikolov quoted in Margarita Kevorkian, "My Life is Creativity," 121. The qualities of the performer-as-co-author that Nikolov valued are also indicated by the composer's comments on the creation of the cello version of *From the Music of Orpheus II*: "Geoffrey Dean...demonstrates not only knowledge of the possibilities of his instrument, but also **creative fantasy and creative talent**." (Lazar Nikolov in a letter to Dimiter Christoff, Sofia, January 28, 2003); my emphasis.
59 Lazar Nikolov quoted in Angelina Petrova, *The Composer Lazar Nikolov*, 271.
60 Hegel, *The Phenomenology of Mind*, trans. J. B. Baillie (NY: Harper and Row, 1967), 229, quoted in Simon Glynn, "Identity, Intersubjectivity and Communicative Action," in *Proceedings of the Twentieth World Congress of Philosophy* (Boston: The Paideia Archive, 1998), 4.

subordinated [to] categories of common action." The analogy principle establishes "the other as another self like myself, a self *like* my self. [It] involves the direct transfer of the meaning 'I.' Like me, my contemporaries, my predecessors, and my successors *can* say 'I.' It is in this way that I am historically related to all the others."[61]

According to Ricoeur, at the heart of Husserl's formulation of "analogical apperception" is the notion of "imaginative transfer. To say that you think as I do, that you experience pleasure and pain as I do, is to imagine what I should think and experience if I were in your place. This transfer in the imagination of my 'here' to your 'there' is the root of what we call empathy (*Einfühlung*)."[62] Husserlian intersubjectivity posits imaginative transfer—a metaphorical "trading places"—as the precondition for achieving understanding.[63] Alessandro Duranti clarifies this point as follows:

> ...the idea is not that we *simultaneously* come to the *same* understanding of any given situation (although this can happen), but that we have, to start, the *possibility* of exchanging places, of seeing the world from the point of view of the Other. Intersubjectivity is thus an existential condition that can *lead* to a shared understanding—an important achievement in its own terms—rather than being itself such an understanding... Husserl recognized intersubjectivity as, first of all, the *possibility* of an understanding, not necessarily its *accomplishment*."[64]

As the "primal experience" in which the possibility of human relationships and communication are grounded, intersubjectivity, according to Alfred Schutz, "is the fundamental ontological category of human existence in the world and therefore of all philosophical anthropology."[65] It is also at the heart of the hermeneutic project: as Ricoeur states, "it is...the growth of his own understanding of himself that he pursues through his understanding of the other. Every hermeneutics is thus, explicitly or implicitly, self understanding by means of understanding others."[66] Orpheus'

---

61 Paul Ricoeur, "Imagination in discourse and action," 127–8.
62 Ibid., 128.
63 Edmund Husserl, *Cartesian Meditations*, trans. D. Cairnes, (The Hague: Nijhoff, 1970), Meditation V.
64 Alessandro Duranti, "Husserl, intersubjectivity and anthropology," *Anthropological Theory*, Vol. 10, no. 1 (2010): 22.
65 Alfred Schutz, "The Problem of Transcendental Intersubjectivity in Husserl," in *Collected Papers*, Vol. 3 (The Hague: Martinus Nijhoff, 1966), 51–83, quoted in Duranti, "Husserl, intersubjectivity and anthropology," 24.
66 Paul Ricoeur, *Hermeneutics and the Human Sciences*, trans. J. B. Thompson (Cambridge: University of Cambridge Press, 1981), 17.

backward glance at Eurydice can be interpreted as just such an intersubjective gesture.

Lazar Nikolov seems to imagine his performer in his own place, as "another self...*like* my self." The power of the projective function of the imagination is paramount in "seeing" the possibility of trading places, of physically being in exactly the same place at the same time, a possibility that is impossible in the physical world, yet serves as the foundation of new meaning. The imaginative transfer of perspectives is central to Nikolov's subconscious use of intersubjectivity in his interactions with the musicians who perform his music. Creative Orphic intersubjectivity can also be reciprocal, as the performer imagines himself in the place of the composer.

As exemplified by Lazar Nikolov's personal vision of Orpheus and by his identification with his performers as musical co-authors, Orphic intersubjectivity provides a way of understanding the composer-performer relationship and can serve as a model for human interaction in musical creativity. I believe that such a model embraces the spirit of the modern hermeneutic tradition, which incorporates reinterpretations of ancient Greek thought and takes its character from the mediating god Hermes.

Chapter 4

Consensual Empathic Manipulation: Listener–Performer Identification and the Interpretative Orphic "I"

Writing in 1962, the American ethnomusicologist Alan Lomax proposed that music research would benefit from a change of orientation, from a departure from traditional formal approaches that studied music "in purely musical terms" in favor of studies that treated "music in context, as a form of human behavior."[1] Lomax followed his own recommendation: comparing the structure of song to the structure of society in world cultures, Lomax's cantometrics theory yielded important insights into the ways music operates in the context of human interaction. Among subsequent scholars who are applying anthropological approaches in their research on music cognition is David Huron, Distinguished Professor at the School of Music and Center for Cognitive and Brain Sciences at Ohio State University. In April 2013 I had the opportunity to attend Huron's keynote address at the 12th International Congress on Music Signification in Louvain-la-Neuve, Belgium. While Huron himself did not use the term on this occasion, I was struck by the implications his ideas have for the role of *empathy* in human interactions through music, suggesting to me that music constitutes more than just a form of behavior in itself: it also embodies other behaviors, including the specific type of empathic behavior that I have termed **consensual empathic manipulation.**

At the outset, it must be agreed that music, understood as a multimodal participatory activity that engages both performers and listeners in equally active ways, *is* indeed a form of human behavior. Once music is acknowledged as a basic form of human interaction—the fact that virtually every culture possesses "something that, from a Western perspective, is recognizable as music"[2] in this participatory sense supports this conclusion—it becomes clear that ideas about human behavior and ideas about music can serve us in a process of mutual illumination. Understanding

---

1   Alan Lomax, "Song Structure and Social Structure," *Ethnology*, Vol. 1, no. 4 (1962): 425.
2   Ian Cross, "Music and Social Being," *Musicology Australia*, 28:1 (2005): 115.

music *as* human interaction leads to greater understanding of human interaction in general. A second prerequisite is that a significant goal of this interaction is to communicate. Like language (but dissimilar to it in important respects), music serves as a mode of communication. Research into the ways that music operates as communication can also point toward ways that music can be intentionally utilized to help influence or develop human behavior.

Huron's research is motivated by the insight that these features of music—as a mode of human behavior and as a mode of communication that influences human behavior—have evolutionary and biological analogues. Inspired by Charles S. Peirce and developed in part from existing studies on animal behavior, Huron's research has identified some of the specific signals and cues that lead to equally specific, correlated emotional responses, and has shown how these signal/response pairs are also valid in musical contexts. It suggests that an identification takes place between a listener and the emotion suggested by a given set of sound qualities expressed and perceived multimodally (as both sound and vision), and that a concurrent identification occurs with the person *producing* those sound qualities. Huron relates these expressed qualities to *cues* that provide information about the organism that produces the cue without that organism intending this. While *cues* are always "honest," *signals* carry the potential for manipulation because they are made with the intent of providing "selected" information to other organisms. A cue, or "honest signal," expresses how one feels, while a signal expresses how one wants someone else to *think* one feels, whether one *actually* feels that way or not.

In this chapter I elucidate concepts related to empathy and empathic response as a ground for demonstrating how empathy, as manifested in the experience of listening to music, operates on the level of *perceived* rather than actual identity as **consensual empathic manipulation.** The music-listening experience takes on the character of a voluntary agreement whereby the listener *expects* the performer to give a dishonest signal, which, when intentionally given, is then intentionally interpreted by the listener *as if* it is honest. I relate this to my idea of co-performative collaboration between composer and performer—what I call **interpretative Orphic intersubjectivity**—as exemplified by my work with the composers Dimiter Christoff and Petros Ovsepyan.

Philosophical and Psychological Theories of Empathy

Briefly stated, empathy is a type of social cognition by which one (the empathizer) identifies with thoughts or feelings of another person (the target), when these thoughts or feelings have not been intentionally communicated by the target. How this actually works, or indeed whether it does work at all, has been the source of much debate among both philosophers and psychologists since the beginning of the twentieth century.

The word "empathy" is an English rendering of the German *Einfühlung* ("feeling into") with origins in the Greek *empatheia*, which initially meant "passion," from *empathēs* ("emotional").[3] This may help explain the frequent emphasis in modern usage on the affective component of empathy and the common confusion or conflation of empathy with affective concepts such as sympathy and compassion. Both sympathy and compassion are more properly understood as examples of specific empathic responses, enabled by but not equivalent to empathy, which can motivate *any* type of interested response.

The rational component of empathy is equally significant for at least three reasons. First, it ensures that the identification with the other is never so extensive that the empathizer loses her autonomous sense of self. This maintenance of objectivity, of a self-recognizing distance from the target, is central to psychologist Heinz Kohut's version of empathy. Particularly in professional contexts such as doctor-patient relationships, it protects the patient (the target) from the kind of affectively-motivated empathic responses that may provide comfort, but do not actually help the patient's recovery.[4] Second, empathy must be at once *more* than just affective identification with the other and *less* than full identification in order to serve as an effective moderator of a well-considered course of action. Finally, the imaginative dimension of empathy is also rational, because it is founded on the acknowledgment that it is not possible to literally share the exact same thoughts and feelings. This is one of the central insights of the imaginative transfer of Husserlian intersubjectivity, discussed in Chapter 3. The word "identification," despite the recommendations offered by many dictionaries, is therefore never fully synonymous with empathy.

---

3 http://www.merriam-webster.com/dictionary/empathy (last accessed January 2, 2015).
4 Heinz Kohut, "Reflections on Empathy," speech given at Self Psychology conference in the University of California at Berkeley, 1981, https://youtu.be/ZQ6Y3hoKI8U (last accessed January 22, 2015).

Jean Decety and Philip L. Jackson report[5] that the necessity of quickly evaluating the motivations of others influenced the evolution of both the organization of neural activity in the brain and the resulting affective communication among both humans and animals. In an evolutionary process guided by the "survival of the fittest" principle, such communication is clearly crucial to basic activities such as food-gathering and reproduction. But, as Decety and Jackson point out, it has not yet been definitively established "how selective pressures tailor such superordinate categories as empathy or social cognition. Selection operates at the level of function, not at the level of physical structures or behaviors that subserve the function. Evolution does not create specific behaviors; it creates mental organizations and inference systems that make people behave in particular ways." Forces that contribute to the evolutionary development of such social cognition systems include the dynamics of the nurturing parent-offspring relationship, increasing social complexity, mastery of the representational properties of language, and "the balance of cost and benefits for the individual who expresses feelings and the observer who interacts with this individual." While social interaction and emotional bonds with others are apparently needed for empathy to develop in the context of an individual human life, it seems likely that empathy is genetically endowed, since there are "evolved biological predispositions (e.g., the capacity to distinguish agents from other objects and to engage in reciprocal interactions with the former but not the latter) that are necessary for the full maturation of empathy."[6]

The German philosopher Theodor Lipps (1851–1914), an early and influential proponent of empathy whose concept of *Einfühlung* is at the heart of his aesthetic theory, believes that empathy enables both "our aesthetic perception and our perception of another embodied person as a minded creature." Lipps writes in 1905 that the nature of aesthetic empathy is always the "experience of another human."[7] As Karsten Stueber explains,

> Empathy in this context is...a phenomenon of "inner imitation," where my mind mirrors the mental activities or experiences of another person based on the observation of his bodily activities or facial expressions. Empathy is ultimately based on an

---

5 Jean Decety and Philip L. Jackson, "The Functional Architecture of Human Empathy," *Behavioral and Cognitive Neuroscience Reviews*, Vol. 3, no. 2 (2004): 71–100.
6 Ibid., 72.
7 Theodor Lipps (1905: 49) quoted in Karsten Stueber, "Empathy," *Stanford Encyclopedia of Philosophy* (2008/2013), http://plato.stanford.edu/entries/empathy/ (last accessed January 22, 2015).

innate disposition for motor mimicry, a fact that is well established in the psychological literature and was already noticed by Adam Smith (1753).[8]

Although Lipps uses the term universally for experiences involving perception of an outside object, his theory of empathy as inner imitation can be seen as a prototype for the simulation theory of empathy (discussed below).[9]

Lipps' ideas were an early challenge to the Cartesian "inference from analogy" theory of understanding other minds that regarded direct and unflawed knowledge of any but one's own mind as something unattainable. According to the phenomenological understanding of empathy expounded by Max Scheler, direct knowledge of the mental states of another *is* possible through observation of physical movements and characteristics—the outward bodily phenomena that express these states. In contrast, the analytical "theory theorists" believe the ability to accurately deduce other's states of mind to be the result of interpreting behavioral clues with a theory, and hold that the apparently direct apprehension of mental states through observation of bodily expressions is the result not of phenomenological fact, but of the observer's knowledge of "folk psychological theory."[10]

Hermeneutic thought rejects empathy insofar as it might be used as a *method* of obtaining understanding in the human sciences because empathy does not account for the cultural embeddedness of the separate agents involved. Following the thought of Heidegger and late Wittgenstein, later philosophers

> think of individual agents as socially and culturally embedded creatures and have started to conceive of the mind of individual agents as being socially constituted. Understanding other agents thus presupposes an understanding of the cultural context within which an agent functions. Moreover, in the interpretive situation of the human sciences, the cultural background of the interpreter and the person, who has to be interpreted, can be very different.[11]

In the realm of psychoanalysis, this limitation of empathy also holds true: "the reliability of empathy declines the more dissimilar the observed is from the observer."[12] Conversely, it can be argued that the *usefulness* of

---

8   Stueber, "Empathy."
9   Ibid.
10 Ibid.
11 Ibid.
12 Heinz Kohut, "Introspection, Empathy, and Psychoanalysis—An Examination of the Relationship Between Mode of Observation and Theory," *Journal of the American Psychoanalysis Association*, 7 (1959): 467.

empathy as a pathway to understanding the other *increases* the more unalike the empathizer and target are.[13]

According to Rameson and Lieberman, the simulation theory of empathy "proposes that we understand the minds of others by using our own mind as a model. By putting ourselves in the 'mental shoes' of another and simulating his or her experience in our own mind, we can intuitively understand what that experience might be like."[14] On the level of neuroscience, this theory is believed to be supported by the results of experiments that have revealed that the same mirror neurons are fired in the brain when one performs an action and when one observes another performing the same action.[15] Simulation theory is sometimes referred to as "simulation-plus-projection."[16]

Some simulation theorists conceive of empathy as a form of mindreading. To account for both the affective and cognitive aspects of empathy, these two aspects are often treated separately. Goldman distinguishes between low-level and high-level mindreading[17] and Stueber between basic and re-enactive empathy, where basic empathy is a mechanism of inner imitation that engages automatically, and re-enactive empathy involves more advanced cognitive processes such as perspective-shifting, imaginative projection, or inferential attribution that allow us to recreate or mimic thoughts occurring in other minds.[18] Decety addresses the low-level and high-level aspects as interacting components of empathy, where "basic," non-intentional motor resonance combines with cognitive insights into the mental state of another that can be intentional, and specifies a third component: the ability to differentiate between self and other.[19]

---

13 C. Daniel Batson, "Empathic Concern and Altruism in Humans," *On the Human* (National Humanities Center, 2009), http://onthehuman.org/2009/10/empathic-concern-and-altruism-in-humans/ (last accessed January 22, 2015).
14 Lian T. Rameson and Matthew D. Lieberman, "Empathy: A Social Cognitive Neuroscience Approach," *Social and Personality Psychology Compass* 3/1 (2009): 95.
15 Rameson and Lieberman,"Empathy: A Social Cognitive Neuroscience Approach," 95.
16 Cf.. Alwin I. Goodman. See Dan Zahavi, "Simulation, projection and empathy," *Consciousness and Cognition* 17 (2008): 114.
17 Alvin I. Goodman, *Simulating minds: The philosophy, psychology, and neuroscience of mindreading* (Oxford: Oxford University Press, 2006), 43, cited in Zahavi, "Simulation, projection and empathy," 515.
18 Zahavi, "Simulation, projection and empathy," 515.
19 Shaun Gallagher, "Empathy, Simulation, and Narrative," *Science in Context*, 25 (2012): 356.

A recurring objection to simulation theory is its first-person starting point.[20] According to Zahavi, recent proponents of the theory such as Goldman and Stueber claim that "empathy is a projective process, in that it involves the imaginative adaptation of another person's point of view or some form of inner or mental imitation." Zahavi concludes that

> simulationism remains stuck in an egocentric predicament. Its focus remains intrapersonal and it is ultimately unable to account for real interpersonal understanding. ...The simulation-plus-projection procedure imprisons me within my own mind...and prevents me from ever achieving a true understanding of *others*.[21]

The imaginative self-projection central to the simulation account of empathy is what C. Daniel Batson calls the "imagine-self perspective," where one imagines how one would think or feel if one were in someone else's place. But Batson sees this type of perspective-taking as the first step toward the more nuanced understanding that comes from what he calls "an imagine-other perspective."[22] This is part of Stueber's re-enactive empathy, which according to Gallagher "requires a higher order simulation of [others'] thoughts or mental states taken as reasons for action [on the part of the empathizer]."[23]

Gallagher and Batson agree that empathic understanding can't be achieved without grasping the *context* of the other's thoughts and feelings. The empathizer seeks to gain "insight into the situation of another person (especially if that person's situation is relatively foreign to us) and into how he or she is affected by that situation."[24] But de Vignemont and Jacob argue that such insight will not be available to the empathizer, who will not have empathized with the target unless this insight into the other's situation engenders *caring* or *concern* in the empathizer. They propose a "caring condition" for empathy requiring that the empathizer must be led, as Gallagher puts it, "to care about the target's affective life because of context." Gallagher suggests "concern condition" as a more parsimonious naming of this condition, because it incorporates the possibility of *negative* concern or interest: "the empathizer must be concerned with the target's affective life because of context."[25]

---

20 This objection occurs regularly in the writings of Gallagher and Zahavi.
21 Zahavi, "Simulation, projection and empathy," 519.
22 Batson, "Empathic Concern and Altruism in Humans."
23 Gallagher, "Empathy, Simulation, and Narrative," 358.
24 Batson, "Empathic Concern and Altruism in Humans."
25 Gallagher, "Empathy, Simulation, and Narrative," 359.

A major theoretical and research focus in empathy studies is on *empathic response*—the type of behavior to which empathy does, or properly should, lead. Using a graphic representation, Rameson and Lieberman contrast four different experiential and propositional processing modes. They suggest that each mode

> represents a unique psychological experience that may hold implications for behavior. For example, adopting an experiential self-focused perspective about a negative event would likely result in personal distress and a desire to avoid the unpleasant stimulus. In contrast, adopting an experiential other-focused perspective would likely result in empathic concern, which might lead to altruistic behavior... Employing propositional, self-focused processing would likely be related to reflecting upon one's own thoughts and feelings about the experience in a metacognitive way.[26]

Batson points out that, apart from empathic concern, the perspective-taking of empathy—when it is understood as interest-motivated mindreading and, as Goldman proposes, its "emotive and caring connotation is bracketed"[27]—can also be used in one of the following self-serving ways:

> to anticipate your opponent's moves and thwart his or her interests, as a skilled chess player or negotiator does...[or] to compare and contrast your reaction to [those of others]. If you judge them to be reacting less appropriately than you think you would—or did—then this form of perspective-taking may provide the basis for censure, condemnation, and rejection. ...**Perspective-taking...is a skill that can be used either to bring us into alignment with the interests of others or to drive us farther apart.**[28]

Regardless of the type of the behavior that empathizing leads to, that behavior must be based on a highly detailed understanding of the other. Psychologist Heinz Kohut, who established "operational empathy" as the primary mode of psychoanalytical observation, explains that

> Introspection and empathy should be looked at as an informer of appropriate action. If you... think yourself appropriately into the inner life of another person, then you can use this knowledge for your purposes. ...These purposes can be of kindness, and these purposes can be of utter hostility. If you want to hurt somebody and you

---

26 Rameson and Lieberman, "Empathy: A Social Cognitive Neuroscience Approach," 102. The authors reference Batson's work on altruistic response (Batson, 1991).
27 Alwin I. Goodman, "Two Routes to Empathy: Insights from Cognitive Neuroscience," in *Empathy: Philosophical and Psychological Perspectives* (Oxford: Oxford University Press, 2011), 4, quoted in Gallagher, "Empathy, Simulation, and Narrative," 357.
28 Batson, "Empathic Concern and Altruism in Humans"; my emphasis.

want to know where his vulnerable spot is, you have to *know* him before you can put in the right dig."[29]

Kohut defines operational empathy as an "extension of introspection (vicarious introspection)." In both scientific psychological analysis and in everyday experience, empathy on Kohut's view is the primary tool used to achieve "psychological understanding." It was through the analyst's empathy with the patient that Freud discovered what Kohut considers to be auxiliary psychoanalytical instruments (resistance, transference, free association, etc.).[30] In my opinion, Kohut's use of empathy *is* empathic in the sense of being motivated by concern: it is applied in psychoanalysis, which has helping the patient as its goal. But Kohut himself shows clear impatience with the "caring" aspect of empathy, because of the tendency to confuse his concept of empathy as a *method*—a mode of observation he sees as unique to psychology—with empathy as a *cure*.

For Paul Ekman, another leading twentieth-century psychologist, an empathic understanding of the other properly leads to compassion, where this term is roughly synonymous with a combination of Batson's empathic concern and the altruistic motivation it engenders. Compassion has been characterized as "the deliberate cultivation of a motivational system, the desire to bring compassion into the world."[31] According to the Dalai Lama, "In Buddhism [compassion] is considered the interdependent nature of one's interests and other's interests, the shared humanity, the fundamental quality of desiring happiness and overcoming suffering."[32]

In outlining specific steps towards achieving compassion as a controllable, lasting state of mind, Ekman draws on his many hours of conversations with the Dalai Lama. Ekman contrasts what he calls identical resonance or affective empathy with reactive resonance or cognitive empathy: empathy is identical when the observer and the target share the same emotion (often referred to as "matching" mental states), and reactive when the observer understands what the target is feeling without sharing the same mental state.[33] The latter is sometimes equated with sympathy, a

---

29   Heinz Kohut, "Reflections on Empathy."
30   Kohut, "Introspection, Empathy, and Psychoanalysis," 461–3.
31   Paul Gilbert, "The Conditions for a Compassionate Society," Empathy and Compassion in Society Conference (London, 2012), https://youtu.be/b3JDokddPts (last accessed January 22, 2015).
32   Dalai Lama quoted in Paul Ekman, "The Roots of Empathy and Compassion," Greater Good Science Center (University of California at Berkeley, 2010), https://youtu.be/3AgvKJK-nrk (last accessed January 22, 2015).
33   Ekman, "The Roots of Empathy and Compassion."

feeling *for* someone else rather than feeling *together with* that person. Elsewhere Ekman elaborates that empathy is "much broader than compassion because compassion is focused on the issue of suffering. ... Compassion is a subset of both the affective and cognitive [empathy] focused on the issue of trying to deal with the suffering of another person. So it's a much narrower slice from the empathic world."[34]

Perceived Authenticity in Music

David Huron's research into multimodal signals investigates on a biological and ethological basis what Scheler's experiential approach to empathy treats phenomenologically. Scheler rejects the idea of simulational projection of one's own thoughts and feelings in favor not only of "expressive phenomena—in particular facial expressions and gestures, but also verbal expressions—[that] can present us with a direct and non-inferential access to the experiential life of others."[35] As Zahavi explains, there is a meeting of self and other that does not blur the boundary between the two as different perspectives. "When I experience the facial expressions or meaningful actions of another, I am *experiencing* foreign subjectivity, and not merely imagining it, simulating it or theorizing about it. I am experiencing the other him- or herself, and not merely some theoretical or imagined construct, some simulation or simulacrum."[36]

It is well established that emotions are linked to specific facial expressions according to biologically and culturally determined rules of display.[37] Inspired by the pioneering work of Charles. S. Peirce and following an ethological model derived from studies of animal behavior, Huron proposes that both empathy and ethological signaling act as "emotional generators" during processes of affective induction such as listening to music.

To gain a fuller understanding of what Huron is suggesting, is it important to set out the accepted features of signaling that have been

---

34 Paul Ekman, "Paul Ekman talks about Empathy with Edwin Rutsch," interview for The Center for Building a Culture of Empathy (2011), https://youtu.be/3i1QFv_PtqM (last accessed January 22, 2015).
35 Zahavi, "Simulation, projection and empathy," 518.
36 Ibid., 520.
37 Paul Ekman, *Emotion in the Human Face: Guide-Lines for Research and an Integration of Findings* (New York: Pergamon, 1972), cited in David Huron, "Understanding Music-Related Emotion: Lessons from Ethology," *Proceedings of the 12th International Conference on Music Perception and Cognition*, ed. P. Cambouropoulos et al. (Thessaloniki, 2012): 478.

identified as applicable not only to interactions among animals, but to human interaction as well. A set of crucial distinctions between signals and cues must be made to allow us to define each in reference to the other:

> A signal is a willing act intended to communicate something to the receiver, whereas a cue informs the receiver without that being the intended goal of the cuer. Signals are cues that are meant to indicate some quality. More precisely, a **signal** is a perceivable action or structure that is intended to or has evolved to indicate an otherwise imperceivable quality about the signaler or the signaler's environment. The purpose of a signal is communication and its goal is to alter the receiver's beliefs or behavior... in ways that benefit the signaler. All **cues** provide a means to infer some quality... Unintentional cues, or evidence, exist for other reasons and they may provide information detrimental to the one who reveals them.[38]

Because signals are meant to be noticed, they rely on what Huron calls redundancy and on sound-size symbolism as observed by Morton and Ohala. In both animal and human behavior, "employing more than one sensory modality makes the signal more conspicuous." Huron gives the example of the human smile as a multimodal signal that is heard as well as seen. Its acoustic properties help explain why, in the case of the smile, the visual element of showing one's teeth is not taken as an indication of aggression.

> Without seeing a person smiling, the smiling is nonetheless evident in the sound of the voice. Flexing the zygomatic muscles characteristic of smiling causes the flesh of the lips to be drawn tight against the teeth. This effectively shortens the length of the vocal tract and so shifts the resonance of the voice upward. In short, the sound of the smile is the sound of a smaller resonant cavity. The upward shift of the spectral centroid is consistent with sound-size symbolism, which, throughout the animal kingdom, is a ubiquitous way of conveying friendly or non-aggressive intent.[39]

The above points to the possibility proposed by Ohala, that the evolutionary origin of the smile is purely auditory, with the visual aspect emerging only later.[40]

The primacy of the auditory component of multimodal signals has also been observed in musical contexts. Huron cites a study by Joseph Plazak that focuses on the perception of sarcasm. When musicians performed during Plazak's experiment in what they thought to be a sarcastic manner, listeners had no difficulty recognizing the musicians' intention without

---

38 Judith Donath, "Signals, cues and meaning," in unpublished book manuscript (2007), 2–3. Quoted with permission of the author.
39 Huron, "Understanding Music-Related Emotion," 474.
40 John J. Ohala, "The acoustic origin of the smile," *Journal of the Acoustical Society of America*, 68, S33 (1980), cited in ibid., 474.

recourse to the visual component. The heightened nasalness of the instrumentalists' musical interpretations, as Huron explains, "approached the "nya nya" timbre associated with vocal taunts characteristic of the sneer or contempt. ...From an ethological perspective, the contempt or sneer facial expression is correlated with a distinctive auditory effect (in this case nasalization). The facial expression and sound go hand-in-hand."[41]

Huron extends these ideas to the perception of music, offering a general Acoustic Ethological Model of signaling that relates combinations of pitch level (high or low) and dynamic (soft or loud) to the quality or type of signal (e.g., friendly or aggressive) being sent. According to this model, high-pitched signals indicate friendliness when they are soft, but convey fear when they are loud. Similarly, softer low-pitched signals show sadness or sleepiness, while louder ones demonstrate aggressive intentions.[42] Huron's own studies have corroborated his model in musical contexts. For example, a female singing higher tones "looks" friendly because her singing is attended by an arrangement of facial features that we are prone to interpret as signaling friendliness. Conversely, the facial expression that occurs naturally when a male vocalist sings low tones is one that we would generally associate with seriousness or even anger.[43]

A distinction must be made between signals that are honest and those that are not. Honest signals resemble cues in several respects. Using the example of the natural facial expressions occurring when a low pitch is sung, we see that the visual component is shaped as the unintentional byproduct of the effort required to produce the sound. Further, a multimodal complex is not being created because there is a resulting non-correspondence between the unintentional facial expression and the expressive intent, for instance in the case of the male singer who may be trying to indicate friendliness with that low pitch, despite the seemingly angry expression we see on his face. If he does not intentionally change his expression to fit the quality of sound, the cue-like signal he sends will be, paradoxically, both honest *and* misleading.

Referring generally to human signaling, Donath states that

> receivers benefit from honest signals, for decisions made and opinions formed with true information are generally better than those that result from false assumptions.

---

41 Joseph Plazak, *Instrumental Irony and the Perception of Musical Sarcasm*, PhD dissertation, School of Music, Ohio State University (2011), cited in ibid., 475.
42 Ibid., 477.
43 David Huron, "Relish and foreboding, pain and pleasure, disappointment and relief: the role of time in hedonic experience," keynote address, 12th International Congress on Music Signification, Louvain-la-Neuve, Belgium, April 2, 2013.

However, signalers sometimes benefit from being dishonest. When the interests of the signaler and the receiver align—when both benefit from honest signaling—we have straightforward, cooperative communication.[44]

In the case of musical performance, I believe there are also benefits to both signaler and receiver from *dishonest* signaling. I am not suggesting that the singer who intentionally shows a friendly face to conform to the character of the sound that he wants to produce (despite making the sound production more difficult by doing so) is being dishonest. The dishonesty—the manipulative content of the signal—emerges when the performer (the signaler) sends signals intended to provoke a specific emotional response in the listener (the receiver) to an emotion that *the performer is not feeling*. The performer's task is to *convey* emotion in such a way that it is perceived by the listener as genuine.

The listener's response to the emotion she *thinks* she hears in the performer's interpretation, signaled by what is heard and usually confirmed by what is seen, is an example of affective empathy in action. The listener identifies with the emotion perceived as belonging to another person. Accordingly, the listener's response to or judgment of the music as an expressive experience is based on the imagined sharing of the emotion *evoked* by the performer as an expressive agent being perceived as *belonging* to that agent. But this empathic response is the result of a signal that is given precisely because the performer *knows* that it will provoke this particular response—a signal that is in effect *dishonest,* because it is given with manipulative intent.

The above seems to imply that the listener's response somehow occurs on its own. But I think it can be argued that the listener, in choosing to listen to *this* music performed by *this* artist, has also chosen the kind of emotional response that she *wants* to have. The act of listening thus represents a kind of contract between performer and listener, in which the parties agree that the performer will play and the listener will allow herself to "be played." I call this agreement **consensual empathic manipulation**.

Huron mentions a survey in which listeners were asked to describe the quality they most admired in their favorite musical artists. The respondents most often used words such as "real," "authentic," and "genuine."[45] So listeners seek what they perceive as authentic, and musicians, knowing that this authenticity is sought, make sure that their performances fulfill that perception. Both parties benefit, although there is

---

44 Donath, "Signals, cues and meaning," 17.
45 Huron, "Relish and foreboding, pain and pleasure."

a marked difference in the *kind* of benefit: the listener benefits emotionally, while the performer, in addition to satisfying an inner need to express herself emotionally, benefits financially.

Each of us is aware, at least subconsciously and at least some of the time, of when we are "being played," when we are allowing ourselves to be manipulated. At times each of us plays the role of manipulator, and in doing so we become savvier in recognizing when others may be manipulating us. John Dewey suggests that this aspect of human behavior is developmentally determined, giving the example of a child who, having learned

> the effect his once spontaneous act has upon those around him...begins to manage and order his activities in reference to their consequences. ...**An activity that was "natural"—spontaneous and unintended—is transformed because it is undertaken as a means to a consciously entertained consequence.**[46]

From a certain point in our lives, to be or not to be manipulated—or manipulative—becomes a conscious choice. In the transition from spontaneous to calculated activity, Dewey locates "art in incipiency."

Interpretative Orphic Intersubjectivity

Multimodal signals have been an acknowledged component in the performance of classical music for centuries. In his *Essay on the True Art of Playing Keyboard Instruments* of 1759, Carl Philipp Emanuel Bach makes unequivocal mention of the necessity to listener perception of what is now known as multimodality in musical performance:

> A musician cannot move others unless he too is moved...In languishing sad passages, the performer must languish and grow sad. Thus will the expression of the piece be more clearly perceived by the audience.... Similarly, in lively, joyous passages, the executant must again put himself into the appropriate mood...**all of this [cannot] be accomplished without gesture**...fitting expressions help the listener to understand our meaning.[47]

Citing later musicians such as the nineteenth-century pianist/composer Franz Liszt and twentieth-century composer Igor Stravinsky, Jane O'Dea asserts that "the conception of the performer "living" the emotions

---

46 John Dewey, *Art as Experience* (New York: Perigee Books, 1934), 62; my emphasis.
47 Carl Philipp Emanuel Bach, *Essay on the True Art of Playing Keyboard Instruments*, trans. W. Mitchell (New York: W. W. Norton, 1949), 152, quoted in Jane O'Dea, *Virtue or Virtuosity? Explorations in the Ethics of Musical Performance* (Westport and London: Greenwood Press, 2000), 56; my emphasis.

enshrined in the musical work is not merely the shallow, cynical philosophy of the exhibitionist showman. It invokes a respected, time-honored tradition in musical performance practice, and one that speaks directly to the interpreter's goal of promoting musical understanding."[48]

In her discussion of the *sensibilité* movement in mid-eighteenth-century Europe, Elisabeth Le Guin posits that rather than understanding, the goal motivating performer and listener alike was to achieve a shared *emotional* experience. This sharing happened through a "crucial maneuver of identification." Le Guin places both performers and audience members in the "receiver" category, and points out that during this period

> the receptive parties to this specular relationship were called on to perform their reception in ways that signaled an ability to feel certain classes of emotion: grief, anguish, ardent love, passionate partisanship. A focal point for such exercises was in the receptive experience of tragedy. ... Women and men alike wept loudly, cried out, buried their faces in their hands, and even fainted in response to the harrowing, elevated dramas appearing on the stage of the Paris Opera. This behavior reached its apex in the 1770s with Gluck's works for that venue [and] is very finely tuned to the drama to which it is a response: take Iphigenia's plight truly and fully to heart, identify yourself with her, and you too will cry out and weep, **as if you were yourself the actress...whom you presume to be similarly transfixed.**[49]

This identification is what Michael Fried refers to as an "absorption" of the receiver into the received.[50] Le Guin points out that "the received" could be a tragic play or opera, a painting, a novel, or—and this is Le Guin's main focus—instrumental chamber music:

> chamber music was chiefly intended for amateur music making, where, as in viewing paintings, one effectively performed for oneself and a few very close associates, themselves absorbed in the act of performance; but with even a few nonplaying listeners in the room, the equation is changed, theatricalized, and the amateur chamber music performer becomes available for *sensible* projection by his listeners. Yet he is not costumed, nor is he veiled by a fictional narrative nor separated from the listeners by a proscenium. The nature of his role is profoundly unclear; he appears to be merely himself. He is engaged in an activity that displays his body in its most exquisite capacity for interactive responsiveness, and without verbal mediation.[51]

What Le Guin calls "the erotic visibility" of instrumental music performance was later rejected as a component of the listening experience. With

---

48 O'Dea, *Virtue or Virtuosity?*, 56.
49 Elisabeth Le Guin, "'One Says that One Weeps, but One Does Not Weep': Sensible, Grotesque, and Mechanical Embodiments in Boccherini's Chamber Music," *Journal of the American Musicological Society* 55 (2002): 209–10; my emphasis.
50 Michael Fried, cited in Le Guin, "'One Says that One Weeps," 210.
51 Le Guin, "'One Says that One Weeps," 212.

the advent of Kantian "disinterested contemplation" and associated "disembodied audience behavior," the listener gradually ceased to perform "the original absorptive maneuver, in which performing bodies were...deliberately conflated with the observer's own."[52]

I revisited these ideas on the plane of composer-performer collaboration as I considered my work with the outstanding Bulgarian composer Dimiter Christoff. In 1999 he asked me to replace the ailing Zdravko Yordanov in the premiere performance of his seven-movement work *Reflections of a Lonely Violoncello* at the Musica Nova Festival in Sofia.[53] In a way I think it could be said that he and I—composer and performer—realized this premiere together. I remember vividly how Professor Christoff described the impressive dramaturgy of this solo cello confession—how, tone by tone, phrase by phrase, we built this drama together, in both sound and gesture. The visual gestures that form an integral part of the interpretation of Christoff's music were developed with the active participation of the composer. He spoke of the "acting out" of the tone sequences found in his scores. The quasi-theatricality of Christoff's interpretative approach was not an external choreography or self-serving virtuosic game—it was the means to an end. Precisely this process of fine-tuning these multimodal gestures with the composer illuminated how movement and sound coexist in his music, leading the performer (me) to the emotional states implied in Christoff's scores and needed for communicating a convincing musical narrative to the listener.

The concept of co-authorship is well-known in musical circles. It presupposes that the performer adds to a lesser or greater extent to the ideas the composer has put forward by, as if the work is created or completed only during its performance on the concert stage. As discussed in Chapter 3, Lazar Nikolov is a conspicuous example in Bulgarian musical culture of a composer explicitly expecting this kind of creative cooperation from those who perform his music. For me, the case of Dimiter Christoff is similar only to the point that he also expects the active cooperation of his performer. In Christoff's case however, this cooperation, and the manner of completion of the composer's Orphic self, are of a different nature, because here the composer takes on a more active and ongoing role

---

52   Ibid., 215.
53   We later collaborated on several other Christoff compositions with cello: *Ricercari* and *The cello abandons the right hand of the piano*, both for cello and piano (with Ganka Nedelcheva); *Jolting further* for cello and harp (with Anna-Maria Ravnopolska); and *I lower my brow* for cello and string orchestra (with Ivan Stoyanov and the Gabrovo Chamber Orchestra).

throughout the rehearsal process in shaping the performer's interpretation of an already-finished musical score. In this type of situation, the composer and performer meet as equals, coming to an agreement about the overall shape of the written work as they prepare it for performance. I propose to codify this kind of collaboration between composer and performer by introducing the concept of the composer as co-performer. It can be also understood in terms of Husserlian imaginative transfer, except that it is operating in the realm of musical *interpretation* rather than creation. I have therefore termed it **interpretative Orphic intersubjectivity.**

My collaboration with the American composer of Armenian origin Petros Ovsepyan in the 1990s can also be characterized as co-interpretive. In Ovsepyan's scores, the suggestion of sound continues over long rests in the score through slow body movements enacted by the performer. These movements are given detailed descriptions in the notation as well as being verbally explained by the author. Christoff's works also make significant, substantive use of silence, notated with fermatas over rests. But while Ovsepyan strictly defines the duration of the implied sound during the rests and often regulates it with an unvaried underlying tempo, each of Christoff's fermatas has a unique, yet unspecified, time value that must be discovered relative to the general flow of the music. And this flow, the natural "breath" of the work is found in the co-performative work with Christoff himself, who otherwise only *encodes* in the musical text the performer's possible physical movements. The co-performance control of Ovsepyan demands strict compliance with the rules of a strictly measured musical score, often in common (4/4) time. Christoff's control leads to an intuitive disclosure of the structure and meaning of the musical text. While Ovsepyan obligates his performer to work as a conduit of sound within a restrictive notated framework, Christoff offers a semblance of freedom from any such framework, allowing his performer to become a narrator, a storyteller in sound.

In terms of the result in performance, the possibility of the performer giving dishonest signals remains. While instructing the performer to "put himself into the appropriate mood," C. P. E. Bach's overarching goal seems to be to lead the listener toward perceiving—if not feeling—a given character or emotion. Similarly, Bach's performer may recognize—and yet not fully feel —the depth of the emotion he is endeavoring to convey through multimodal means. For the proponents of sensibilité, the goal seems to have been similar: a complete emotional identification with the sentiments of the music, enacted as a kind of co-performance along with the performer, whom the listener "presumes to be similarly transfixed." In the case of Christoff's music, performer and listener can similarly be grouped together as receivers: "the music of Dimiter Christoff develops new sensibilities and skills in the performer and listener alike."[54]

In the foregoing I have demonstrated that empathy, as manifested in the experience of listening to music, operates on the level of *perceived or presumed identification* in a type of interactive human behavior that I call **consensual empathic manipulation.** The performer creates conditions that will cause that perception to take place. The listener interprets the dishonest signal *as if* it is honest, because the benefits of "being played" outweigh any potential harm that could come from this temporary identification with another.

---

54 Elizaveta Vulchinova-Chendova, "Muzikata na Dimiter Christoff kato sugestivna "vuobrazhaema mnogolineinost": prostranstvo ot strukturirani i razgurnati zvukovi arhetipi," *Bulgarsko muzikoznanie (Bulgarian Musicology)* 3–4 (2013): 201–26; my translation.

Part III

Ensemble Ethics

Chapter 5

Cultural Values in Music: Control and Conversation in String Quartet Playing

There has been what I consider to be a shift toward communitarian values in the orientation of recent philosophical thinking on music. With reference to MacIntyre's definition of social practice, Small's concept of "musicking," and Gadamer's interrelated concepts of "play" and "festival," in this chapter I discuss how more culturally-inclusive views of music frame music as a social practice where the once-primary concept of the work is subsumed in the event and its attendant human relationships.

Turning my attention to classical music in the Western tradition, I inquire as to the human relationships that might be required for a performance that is satisfactory to all participants, regardless of their role. From a nineteenth-century utopian vision of a town where music is the only profession to more recent examples, I examine how musical practices both embody certain types of relationships and model social practices outside the realm of music. I contrast the communitarian values suggested by the conductor's control of orchestral musicians who submit to that control for the good of the music to the more liberal bias of the collaborative, team-oriented decision-making of orchestras and chamber ensembles working without a conductor.

I propose that two similarly opposing, yet overlapping approaches to human interaction—I term them the **conversation and control models**—lie at the origins of the quintessential classical chamber music genre, the string quartet, permeating the music itself and coloring the relationships among the musicians who perform it. After looking at historical precedents from late eighteenth- and early nineteenth-century Vienna and examining enduring elements of the two models, I consider their relevance to my own experience as an American member of two leading professional string quartets whose other members were all Bulgarian.

Play, Festival, and Musicking

As I demonstrated in Part I, the aesthetics of Heidegger, Dewey, and Gadamer anticipate a more recent mainstream philosophical approach to music, in which the musical work is decentered and music is understood as a type of human experience. The work as the autonomous product of an individual's imagination and existing before it is performed gives way to the view that the work exists to give musicians something to perform,[1] and has no meaning until it fulfills this social function in actual practice. Although Nicholas Wolterstorff and others who conceive of music in terms of "the social *practices* of art…the *interplay* between works, practices, and participants in these practices"[2] do not mention the connection, I would argue that this conception is very similar to the Gadamerian concept of the "hermeneutic identity" of the work of art and the conditions for achieving it, as discussed in Chapter 2.

Wolterstorff does refer extensively to Alasdair MacIntyre's analysis of the concept of social practice in elucidating some of its important features. These features can be regarded as communitarian in their reference to others rather than to self. According to MacIntyre, a social practice is a kind of activity that

- requires new practitioners to learn skills taught by modelling or receiving instruction from others;
- requires them to join a group of existing practitioners, who may be instructed by more experienced practitioners and non-practitioners;
- has a history and traditions, standards of excellence, set rules, and records of achievement that go along with them.[3]

A social practice, then, is one in which the practitioner engages with others. MacIntyre himself emphasizes this element of developing relationships among the participants in a practice: "to enter into a practice is to enter into a relationship not only with its contemporary practitioners, but also with those who have preceded us in the practice, particularly those

---

1 Christopher Small, *Musicking: The Meanings of Performing and Listening* (Middletown, CT: Wesleyan University Press, 1998), 9.
2 Nicholas Wolterstorff, "The Work of Making a Work of Music," in *What is Music? An Introduction to the Philosophy of Music*, 109; his emphasis.
3 Wolterstorff, "The Work of Making a Work of Music," 109–10.

whose achievements extended the reach of the practice to its present point."[4]

Christopher Small has characterized the social practice of music as "part of that larger dramatic enactment which we call ritual, where the members of the community acted out their relationships and their mutual responsibilities and the identity of the community as a whole was affirmed and celebrated." He continues:

> In the culture of villages, as well as of those quite small cities (by present-day standards), from ancient Athens to eighteenth-century Vienna, which up to the recent past have formed centers of urban culture, performers and audience have known one another as members of the same community. Most of the world's population lived in villages, where...music specialists were socially necessary for the central part they played in the rituals of the community that celebrated the mythologies of birth, marriage, death, harvest and the other great events of life. Since everyone took part in the singing and the dancing, the distinction between performers and listeners was generally blurred...just sitting and silently contemplating the performance was no part of the experience.[5]

In a musical performance that takes place in a concert hall, the roles of the various participants are much more clearly defined and delineated, and the participants in these roles are often unknown to each other. Even so, the event itself can still be seen in terms of social practice and the attendant human interaction and relationships. To capture this sense of music as an activity—as a shared experience—Small proposes the verb "musicking," applying it not only in the sense of "to perform" or "to make music," but far more broadly, defining "to music" as *"to take part, in any capacity, in a musical performance, whether by performing, by listening, by rehearsing or practicing, by providing material for performance (what is called composing), or by dancing."* According to Small's definition, the activity of anyone who is "contributing to the nature of the event that is a musical performance" is musicking.[6] It is an inclusive, descriptive term rather than a prescriptive one: it implies no value judgments. Small's theory of musicking favors music as action and does not privilege any participant or role in the activity. Most significantly, it emphasizes the human relationships: "whatever it is that we are doing, we are all doing it together."[7]

---

4 Alasdair MacIntyre, *After Virtue* (Notre Dame, IN: University of Notre Dame Press, 1984), 181, quoted in Wolterstorff, "The Work of Making a Work of Music," 109.
5 Small, *Musicking,* 39–40.
6 Ibid., 9; Small's emphasis.
7 Ibid., 10.

The philosophical reorientation from the art of music to the social practice of musicking has in my opinion a clear theoretical antecedent in the aesthetics of Gadamer, who has been described as the "greatest recent German philosopher who might be called communitarian."[8] This connection is especially apparent in Gadamer's concepts of *play* and *festival*. Gadamer updates and broadens the sense of play as it had been used by Friedrich Schiller. For Schiller, the subject who "plays" acts alone, autonomously, in an imaginary realm outside his normal realm of experience. According to Jean Grondin, Gadamer's play of art is also a "playing along" or "playing with" in which "the subject is not restricted to himself, nor is he freed from his theoretical and practical expectations. ...The observer of an artwork is interwoven into an event that he does not control and in which he cannot freely dispose of his normal horizons of experience and expectations."[9] Whereas Schiller's play is "playful," Gadamer's play is serious, because to play along implies a kind of participation in which our whole being is at stake.

The element of participation—of "playing together" in this serious sense—is central to Gadamer's related concept of festival. A festival is an act that brings people together, in which the sense of belonging to the "festive community" becomes more significant, and is ultimately more memorable to the participants, than the actual content of the event. It is a shared experience that involves practitioners of a given social practice. Musicking is just such a festive act, where what is crucial is not that something is being done, but that "we are all doing it together."

The active togetherness of the Gadamerian festival also ties its participants to tradition: a festival is itself a recurring event. In MacIntyre's view, tradition is an authority that one must confront and learn from. Gadamer makes a similar assertion:

> As finite beings we stand in traditions, whether we know these traditions or not, whether we are conscious of them or so blinded as to believe that we begin anew. This does not affect at all the power of tradition over us. However, it does make a difference if we face the traditions in which we stand and the future possibilities that they preserve for us, or whether one conceitedly imagines that one could turn away from the future into which one is living and program and constitute ourselves in a

---

8   Kelvin Knight, "Aristotelianism versus Communitarianism," *Analyse & Kritik* 27 (2005): 260. Cf. David Ingram, *Reason, History, and Politics: The Communitarian Grounds of Legitimation in the Modern Age* (Albany: State University of New York Press, 1995).

9   Jean Grondin, "Play, Festival and Ritual in Gadamer: On the theme of the immemorial in his later works," in *Language and Linguisticality in Gadamer's Hermeneutics* (Lanham, MD: Lexington Books, 2001), 43.

new way. Clearly tradition does not mean mere conservation, but rather a passing along, but this includes that one does not leave things unchanged and merely conserved, but that one says anew and learns to grasp anew something old.[10]

Gadamer is clearly rejecting the possibility of self-determination, of being able to "turn away from the future into which one is living." To him, our embeddedness in tradition and community are not choices: they are facts of being. To imagine otherwise, to suppose that we are "self-conscious, autonomous beings, who control their time and direct their life," argues Grondin, is to forget "how much tradition and not-knowing belong to our fate."[11] This "other-determinedness" is an element common to both Small's musicking and Gadamer's play and festival concepts.

Small asserts that "a musical performance, while it lasts, brings into existence relationships that model in metaphoric form those which [the participants] would like to see in the wider society of their everyday lives."[12] Elsewhere he distinguishes two sets of relationships that exist while a musical performance is in progress: "those between the sounds that are made in response to the instructions given in the score and those between the participants in the performance. These two sets of relationships...are themselves related."[13] Both sets perform two different functions: they are metaphorically *modelling* relationships that *might* exist in other social practices, and they are *exemplifying* relationships that *do* exist in the social practice of musicking. Following Wolterstorff's suggestion that the social realities of a composer's time serve as a guide during the creative process and "become embodied in the works,"[14] I would argue that at least two more sets of relationships are "in play." When the composer is not contemporary with the performance, musicking also exemplifies relationships that *formerly* existed, both in the social practice of musical performance and in society in general. In such cases, this in turn implies a fourth function, that of *mediating* between existing and once-existing relationships in a way that might be likened to Gadamer's fusion of horizons.

---

10 Hans-Georg Gadamer, *The Relevance of the Beautiful and Other Essays*, ed. R. Bernasconi, trans. N. Walker (Cambridge: Cambridge University Press, 1986), 138f, quoted in Grondin, "Play, Festival and Ritual in Gadamer," 50: n.
11 Grondin, "Play, Festival and Ritual in Gadamer," 48.
12 Small, *Musicking*, 46.
13 Ibid., 138–9.
14 Wolterstorff, "The Work of Making a Work of Music," 108.

Communitarian Conceptions of Musical Utopia

It has been proposed that the origins of an "authentic communitarianism" might be traced to "Romanticism's celebration of the social constitution of the self and of the self's expression of itself as so constituted, including its patriotic identification with its particular community in rivalry with other communities."[15] It was during the nineteenth century—the period of musical Romanticism—that a kind of "religion of art" developed and artists "gave Art for the first time its capital A. Art was the highest conceivable expression of man. Art was the infallible critic of life and society."[16] One of the most important adherents to this "religion" was the French composer Hector Berlioz (1803–1869), who is also known for his erudite writings on music and society. In his 1854 essay "Euphonia,"[17] set five centuries in the future, Berlioz employs metaphors drawn from music as both art and practice to outline his utopian vision of a community where music-making is the primary social practice. By negative reference, Berlioz also comments on the musical practices of his own time, both documenting and critiquing them. His suggestions for new inventions to aid musical study and performance apply the potential of then-new technology to perfecting musical instruments and improving the efficiency of interactions among musicians.

Berlioz likens the social structure of the town of Euphonia (population 12,000) to "a great Conservatory of music" because the occupations of its inhabitants are all related to the art of music. "Most of them are both instrumentalists and singers. A few who do not perform music devote themselves to the manufacture of instruments or to the engraving and printing of music. Others give their time to acoustical research and to the study of that branch of physics which relates to the production of sound." Like the organization of a symphony orchestra, the geographical layout of the various districts of Euphonia categorizes its citizens according to the instruments they play.[18]

Berlioz states that the form of government in Euphonia is—and must be, according to him—military and despotic, with a benevolent emperor providing for the happiness of all Euphonians. Here the presence of an

---

15 Kelvin Knight, "Aristotelianism versus Communitarianism," 259.
16 Jacques Barzun, "Berlioz as man and thinker," in *The Cambridge Companion to Berlioz*, ed. P. Bloom (Cambridge: Cambridge University Press, 2000), 13.
17 Hector Berlioz, "Euphonia, or The Musical City," in *Evenings with the Orchestra*, trans. and ed. J. Barzun (New York: Alfred A. Knopf, 1956), 258–97.
18 Berlioz, "Euphonia, or The Musical City," 283.

authoritarian regime—generally regarded as a negative potential outcome of communitarian thinking—is taken as a given that ensures "perfect order... and the marvelous results...for art."[19] Similarly, Berlioz proposes a process for preparing musical compositions for performance that gives the composer full control over how his music will sound, as well as a new invention that allows him, as the conductor of the performance, to literally "play" the orchestra. All the skills and resources required for the social practice of music are placed entirely at the service of the musical equivalent of the benevolent dictator.

Throughout the essay, the citizens are treated as a unified, yet passive group. All are given the same musical training, and if anyone's personal judgment is found to be at odds with "truth of expression"—the highest Euphonian aesthetic value—he is "inexorably banished from the city, however eminent his talent or exceptional his voice,"[20] in an obvious privileging of one's usefulness to the group over one's personal qualities. The citizens have responsibilities, but no stated rights. They are "trained to [keep] silence,"[21] and when Berlioz writes that every Euphonian "has some kind of voice," it is only to state that all are therefore required to sing. They must all have the same musical skills, and figuratively they must all have the same opinion. In both senses, all Euphonians "sing the same song." The whole population is in attendance when solo performers are chosen, but the composers, ministers and prefects set the criteria and make the selections based on suitability, not social status, suggesting that connections with those in power are not an advantage. In Euphonia, "no privileges are granted any artists to the detriment of art."[22]

Berlioz's vision of a self-contained community in which music is the only profession suggests a set of ideal relationships that, if they did exist, could conceivably benefit everyone involved in music-making, at least in the sense of making the most satisfactory music. Berlioz presupposes that the rank-and-file musicians will unconditionally accept being controlled by a dictator-like conductor, making it clear that true Euphonians would make any necessary personal sacrifice—and would not even frame such deprivations as sacrifices at all—in the name of art. Serving art is the common purpose, the ultimate common good, of this community. The

---

19 Ibid., 283.
20 Ibid., 284.
21 Ibid., 286.
22 Ibid., 288–9.

conductor-dictator is tolerated, and possibly idolized, because he too is seen as sacrificing self for art.

The idolization of the conductor—a role in musical performance that Berlioz championed—can also be observed among modern concertgoers, who hold the conductor in "somewhat disproportionate regard," considering that she alone among the performing musicians produces no sound. The distinguished twentieth-century composer Paul Hindemith saw the conductor's visible demeanor on the concert podium as a "demonstration of some refined and stylized form of oppression" in which the listener "enjoys the perfect abreaction of his own suppressed feelings." An identification takes place during the performance between the despotic behavior that the conductor is perceived to be displaying and the individual's "most natural human desire of governing, ordering, dictating to, and even torturing his fellow men."[23] In this way the activities of the conductor become a kind of vicarious wish-fulfillment for the listener, as long as the concert lasts.

Here Hindemith is referring specifically to the enjoyment of watching the conductor, and not necessarily connecting that enjoyment to any pleasure derived from the music that is being made by the orchestra under the conductor's direction. It seems highly unlikely that any reasonable person, even one who did derive pleasure from identifying with a despotic conductor, would want to see precisely this relationship exist in his everyday life, because she assumes that such despotic behavior would never be tolerated outside the context of the musical performance, and therefore would never achieve the same "harmonious" result.

Hindemith is also writing in an era when the authoritarian conductor was widely regarded as a particularly successful type of leader, one capable of unifying the individual members of the orchestra to shape a convincing interpretation of the music performed. Other conducting types have also been delineated, and their approaches to leading the orchestra have been drawn on as models for managing a team in a contemporary business environment. In his role as a consultant to businesses, conductor Itay Talgam has analyzed the performances of some of the outstanding orchestral conductors of the past in search of models for human interaction in the office and marketplace. Tellingly, the management model he recommends to business leaders is exemplified by the "enabling" leadership approach of conductor Carlos Kleiber, whose positive spirit of teamwork

---

23 Paul Hindemith, *A Composer's World: Horizons and Limitations* (Mainz: Schott Musik International, 1952), 106.

motivates each member of the orchestra to do his best work, to "tell his own story." Kleiber supports the player's efforts through positive reinforcement rather than overtly controlling them. But it is control nonetheless because the player knows he will be rewarded with a pleased look and more freedom in individual interpretation if he performs well, and sanctioned with a displeased look and increased outside control over his interpretation if he does not.[24] Conformity to the same high musical standards is expected by both despotic and enabling conductors, but the enabler's approach seems to have more potential for direct application to social practices outside the realm of music.

Another model drawn from musical interaction and applied to business contexts involves ensembles that operate without a conductor, among which the Orpheus Chamber Orchestra of New York City takes high rank. This conductorless orchestra is by no means leaderless, but the leaders come from among the orchestra's players and are rotated on a regular basis to allow the interpretation of any given composition to change and evolve. Their approach to preparing music for performance is based on "the sharing of leadership, the taking of individual responsibility, and the literal movement of players to fit the musical sound."[25] Each player in the orchestra has the right to stop the group during rehearsal to make suggestions for improving the interpretation. A small number of core players (also rotating) is given more responsibility to keep rehearsals as efficient as possible while preserving the spirit of dialogue. Thus "the best thinking of virtuoso musicians blends into something more than one person could envision." This kind of collective decision-making can be contrasted to the way the interpretation is shaped in conductor-led rehearsals. Whatever type of leader a conductor may be, "the large orchestra is built around the notion that the conductor's authority is absolute. If he/she were ever to accept advice or a suggestion from a member of the orchestra, it would have to be done in private. Any other scenario would suggest weakness."[26]

The Orpheus Chamber Orchestra's approach to music-making works both ways. It has been appropriated in business circles to challenge the conventional wisdom that "somebody has to be in charge," but at the same time Orpheus musicians use business metaphors: "at this level of

---

24 Itay Talgam, "Lead like the great conductors," TEDtalk (2009), http://www.ted.com/talks/itay_talgam_lead_like_the_great_conductors.html (last accessed January 22, 2015).
25 John Lubans, Jr., "The Invisible Leader: Lessons for Leaders from the Orpheus Chamber Orchestra," *OD Practitioner*, Vol. 38, no. 2 (2006): 7.
26 Orpheus Chamber Orchestra musicians, quoted in ibid., 7.

participation," says one, "we own the company." Lubans suggests the Orpheus approach is at once a *model* that can be applied in non-musical contexts and an *actualization* of a general management theory in which leaders and followers alike are, as Mary Parker Follet puts it, "following the invisible leader—the common purpose."[27]

Core Values in String Quartet Performance Traditions

The skills the members of the Orpheus Chamber Orchestra employ—"listening closely, knowing when to lead, and when to follow, approaching performance with a collaborative spirit"—are the same skills that are learned through the preparation and performance of chamber music.[28] Broadly defined, chamber music is music performed without a conductor, but the main categories of chamber music compositions are ensembles with ten or fewer players (compared to as many as fifty or sixty in a chamber orchestra), in which each individual part in the written musical score is played by a single player (not by sections of players as in the orchestra). Chamber music (*musica da camera*) takes its name both from the small number of players and the intimate spaces (chambers) in which it was first performed. The string quartet, a four-member chamber ensemble consisting of two violins, viola, and cello, is widely regarded as the quintessential classical chamber music medium for compositions in the string quartet genre.

The string quartet emerged during the mid-eighteenth century as a kind of "music of friends." Early documented quartet performances took place in private homes, sometimes with only the players themselves in attendance, and sometimes with a select audience hardly larger than the players in number. A well-known example is the February 1785 gathering of five in Vienna, when the composer himself was among the four players who played through three of Wolfgang Amadeus Mozart's new string quartets. Mozart dedicated these compositions to an older Viennese composer, Joseph Haydn, who is often credited with having a leading role in originating the string quartet genre two decades earlier. Haydn also

---

27 Mary Parker Follet, quoted in ibid., 6.
28 Robert Gibson quoted in "Orpheus Chamber Orchestra and Morton Subotnick in Residence at the University of Maryland," University of Maryland College of Music news item (April 15, 2011), http://www.music.umd.edu/news/post/256 (last accessed January 22, 2015).

participated in the February 1785 reading.[29] It was on this occasion that Haydn declared to Mozart's father Leopold "before God, as an honest man, that your son is the greatest composer I know either personally or by reputation. He has taste as well as a consummate knowledge of the art of composition."[30]

Over the course of the eighteenth century there was a marked development of musical competence among European concertgoers. As they became increasingly knowledgeable in music theory and skilled as amateur performers, the expectation arose for professional composers to "consider them not as passive receivers but as active partners in the process of communication, and thus to engage them in a game played upon the technical rules of composition… suggest[ing] that, within the metaphor of language, the ancient model of oration gradually gave way to a more modern ideal of conversation."[31]

This new "ideal of conversation" is clearly reflected in a statement by Goethe, who famously wrote that in a string quartet, "One hears four intelligent people conversing with one another, believes one might learn something from their discourse and recognize the special characteristics of their instruments."[32] Two distinct types of conversation are in evidence here: among the four instruments of the string quartet, and between composer and listener. Goethe seems to betray a liberal bias, referring to "four intelligent people" as individuals rather than as a group and to "the special characteristics" of the individual instruments, revealed to him through the performance of the musical composition. There is no implication of a social hierarchy: the four are equals.

Haydn and Mozart both engaged in non-musical social practices that may be reflected in the nature of their private chamber music gatherings and in the rational, individualistic content of their string quartet compositions. At the time of the February 1785 read-through of Mozart's "Haydn" quartets, four of the participants—Haydn, Mozart, and the two Barons Tinti—were initiated Freemasons, and Mozart's father was initiated soon thereafter.[33] Maynard Soloman explains that unlike other Freemason

---

29   Christina Bashford, "The String Quartet and Society," in *The Cambridge Companion to the String Quartet*, ed. R. Stowell (Cambridge: Cambridge University Press, 2003), 3–5.
30   Paul Nettl, *Mozart and Masonry* (New York: Philosophical Library, 1957), 33.
31   Agawu Mirka, *Communication in Eighteenth-Century Music* (Cambridge: Cambridge University Press, 2012), 2.
32   Johann Wolfgang von Goethe, quoted in William Drabkin, *A Reader's Guide to Haydn's Early Quartets* (Greenwood Publishing Group, 2000), 3.
33   Nettl, *Mozart and Masonry*, 30–33.

members who delved into the occult, Mozart was a member of the Freemason movement's rationalist, Enlightenment-inspired faction known as the Illuminati.[34] Founded in 1776 by University of Ingoldstadt professor of canon law Adam Weishaupt, a personal acquaintance of Mozart's, the Illuminati shared the humanist views of the French encyclopedists Rousseau and Diderot, who contended that nobility of spirit was not contingent on social rank. The Illuminati had grown out of Weishaupt's secretive meetings with his university students in Bavaria: "They assembled in a private apartment, and there he discussed with them philosophic subjects, and sought to imbue them with a liberal spirit. This was the beginning of the Order of the Illuminati, or the Enlightened—a name he bestowed upon his disciples as a token of their advance in intelligence and moral progress."[35] The Freemasons believed that music should "inculcate feelings of humanity, wisdom and patience, virtue and honesty, loyalty to friends, and finally an understanding of freedom."[36]

As a "music of friends," I would argue that the string quartet of the 1780s shared much with freemasonry as a social practice. Like the public figures who joined the freemason movement, the quartet players were like-minded people who met behind closed doors. Both groups aspired to be enlightened, rational thinkers. In translating that thinking into musical action, they chose musical "conversation topics" of interest both to themselves and to their enlightened listeners, and they wove these topics into "an intimate and tightly constructed dialogue among equals."[37]

The writings of composer and music critic Johann Friedrich Reichardt significantly enhance the picture of the liberalistic origins of the string quartet in the social milieu of late eighteenth-century Vienna. Of a December 1808 Viennese string quartet concert series, Reichardt comments, "difficult as it is to bring this sort of music to perfection in performance—for the whole and each of its single parts are heard in their entirety...—it is the first variety to be provided wherever good friends of music meet to play together."[38] Reichardt offers important insights into the nature of

---

34 Maynard Solomon, *Mozart: A Life* (New York: HarperCollins, 2009), 467.
35 Albert G. Mackey, "Weishaupt" and "Illuminati of Bavaria" in *Encyclopedia of Freemasonry*, Vol. 2 (1878).
36 Ludwig Friedrich Lenz: *Freymäurer-Lieder* (Altenburg, 1746), 34–36.
37 Bashford, "The String Quartet and Society," 4.
38 Johann Friedrich Reichardt, from *Briefe geschrieben auf einer Reise nach Wien* in *Source Readings in Music History: The Classic Era*, ed. O. Strunk (New York: Norton, 1965), 154–66.

chamber music as social practice, as he observed and understood it. I summarize his observations below:

- The concerts were "opened by subscription" (i.e., admission was charged).
- The concerts took place in a private house.
- The audience was small and "consisted entirely of ardent and attentive friends of music."
- This type of audience is considered by Reichardt "precisely the proper public for this most elegant and most congenial of all musical combinations" (i.e., the string quartet).
- Each player "takes at least some degree of pleasure in the performance, once he has brought to it all that he can offer it individually or through his immediate background."
- Because of the technical difficulty of achieving "the most perfect intonation, ensemble, and blending" within the group, the "over-trained" ears of enlightened listeners and critics might not find the performance very pleasurable.

Reichardt dwells at length on the specific string quartet concert he attended. Finding the ensemble to be "on the whole well balanced," he praises first violinist Ignaz Schuppanzigh, whose "capricious manner of performance" Reichardt finds appropriate for the quartets of Haydn, Mozart, and Beethoven, but notes that the "local virtuosi" have better intonation than Schuppanzigh, who "plays the most difficult passages clearly, though not always quite in tune." He credits Schuppanzigh's leadership of "his carefully chosen colleagues" for the way they "enter admirably into the spirit of the composer."[39]

What follows in Reichardt's account is an extended critique of one overbearing feature of Schupannzigh's leadership: his "accursed fashion...of beating time with his foot." Reichardt details how this habit adversely affects the quality of the individual players' execution of their parts in the performance, where "it is far better to let a mistake pass without censure, whether actually committed or only feared, than to try to help matters by using strong measures." He also describes how it negatively impacts the audience's experience, distorting it for the listener: "Generally speaking, one seldom hears a forte here—let alone a fortissimo—without the leader's joining in with his foot. For me this ruins the pure free enjoyment, and every such beat interrupts for me the coordinated and perfected

---

39 Ibid., 159–60.

performance which it is supposed to help bring about and which I had expected from this public production."⁴⁰

In reaching his conclusion about controlling behavior similar to that of Hindemith's despotic conductor, Reichardt offers a pointed assessment of quartet playing as a group practice *of individuals*, each of whom needs his *own space within which to operate* to achieve an optimal performance.

> Furthermore, an attentive and conscientious colleague ought never to be disconcerted by such shameful public prompting—it can only disturb his repose and self-control, on which above all the perfection of the performance depends; an inattentive and sluggish colleague ought not to count on so ordinary means of assistance and stimulation. Each one must help with all his senses and his entire attention; he who is incapable of this cannot be trained to it by beating time.⁴¹

What I term the **conversation model** of string quartet music-making, with its origins in the Masonic friendships of the Viennese musical circle of Haydn and Mozart, is based on preponderantly liberal values. It relies on the free exchange of individual opinions to reach a common goal. The model imposed by Schuppanzigh's foot—I call it the **control model**—alters the balance of the relationships among the participants toward communitarian values and a potentially totalitarian outcome: individuality is suppressed in the name of the common good and a leader emerges to enforce that suppression.

Just as communitarian thinking does not necessarily exclude liberal values, the two models are not mutually exclusive. Variations on and combinations of the two models continue to permeate the traditions of string quartet preparation and performance, contributing to the uniqueness of the approach and sound of different ensembles working in the string quartet medium. The conversation and control models correspond in large measure to what have been identified as "two subtly different styles of string quartet performance": the American and European styles.⁴²

While most ensembles would probably agree on the string quartet performance goals Reichardt enumerated—perfect intonation, ensemble, and blending—it is important to clarify that the first two goals are more objective in that certain accepted standards can be applied to aurally perceiving what is in or out of tune and what is or is not together in time.

---

40 Ibid., 159.
41 Ibid., 159.
42 J. Keith Murnighan and Donald E. Conlon, "The Dynamics of Intense Work Groups: A Study of British String Quartets," *Administrative Science Quarterly*, Vol. 36, no. 2 (1991): 166.

Blending is a much more subjective category, because while the amount of blending among the instruments—to what extent the individual parts are heard as separate strands in the texture, or to what extent the quartet sounds as if the four instruments are playing "as one"—is also perceptible, there is considerable fluctuation as to how *much* blending is needed at different moments in the music. Intonation and ensemble are the constants, while blending—maintaining a satisfactory balance among the individual parts—is the main variable in shaping a unique and compelling interpretation of a composition in the string quartet genre.

The *manner* and *degree* of blending is a major feature distinguishing the American style of string-quartet playing from the European. "Sounding as one" is associated with European quartet playing, while an approach in which "the quartet sounds like four voices, combined harmoniously; the members retain their individuality but relate to each other's sound in an organized way" is recognized as American.[43] The following press quotes, from reviews of performances by the aptly-named American Quartet, an ensemble of American-trained players based in New York City, confirm the wider and enduring acceptance of the American/European differentiation: "[a] combination of individual brilliance and ensemble perfection" (*Darmstädter Echo*); "Americans certainly, but with a refined European style" (*Giornale de Sicilia*).[44]

In recent decades increasing attention has been focused on how the string quartet functions as a social unit. It has been referred to as a self-regulating organization[45] and studied as a type of self-managing team[46] or Intense Work Group.[47] Murnighan and Conlon identify the following characteristics that mark string quartets as intense work groups:

> Members are reciprocally interdependent..., using each other's outputs as their own inputs, and vice versa. Their interdependence is also complete and immediate: Their work is done only as a unit; they cannot perform a string-quartet composition without all of the members working together simultaneously. They are artists who collaborate; they must simultaneously devote their concentration to their own and to each other's playing. Many quartet players commented in the interviews that the ability to listen and respond to each other was the most important characteristic that

---

43 Ibid., 166.
44 American Quartet reviews, http://www.americanstringquartet.com/reviews.htm (last accessed January 22, 2015).
45 Bashford, "The String Quartet and Society."
46 See Avi Gilboa and Malka Tal-Shmotkin, "String quartets as self-managed teams: An interdisciplinary perspective," *Psychology of Music*, Vol. 40, no. 1, (2012): 19–41.
47 See Murnighan and Conlon, "The Dynamics of Intense Work Groups."

differentiated quartet players from soloists... Their collective task is to reach a high level of coordinated sound.[48]

Discussing how an ensemble can take root in a community and nurture its musical and professional development, first violinist Nicholas Kitchen of the Boston-based Borromeo Quartet confirms that the collective work of a string quartet is self-regulating. "Ensembles tend to pressure their members to aspire to ever higher standards and, though this can cause internal tension, it tends to work. This quartet's steady improvement then inspires all those around them and creates a virtuous cycle from which everyone can benefit."[49]

The juxtaposition of liberal and communitarian values found in a string quartet as a social unit results in part from the particular combination of ages, musical training, cultural backgrounds, and personal relationships among its members. Even renowned quartets whose members have similar training and backgrounds do not necessarily get along, as the famous example of the Budapest String Quartet, whose members insisted on staying in separate hotels while on tour, attests. Quartets such as the Tokyo (originally all Japanese members) and the Shanghai (originally all Chinese) are perceived as having unique approaches to music-making in part because of their unified cultural backgrounds. The same holds true for quartets consisting of members of the same family, such as the Hagen Quartet of Austria (siblings) and the Ying (also siblings) and Jupiter Quartets (siblings and spouses) in the United States.

Borodin Quartet founding first violinist Rostislav Dubinsky, with whom I studied chamber music at the Indiana University School of Music, complained that his quartet could never achieve the sound he wanted because the Soviet government had replaced his original Jewish colleagues in the quartet with non-Jewish ones who did not have the same inherent understanding of string-instrument playing as he and therefore were not already seeking the same kind of sound or interpretation. He countered this perceived problem through his role as artistic director of the quartet, which put him in charge of the rehearsal process and decisions, from the shaping of the musical interpretations to how much time would be spent on each composition. Dissenting opinions within the ensemble were seen as

---

48 Murnighan and Conlon, "The Dynamics of Intense Work Groups," 165–6. The authors reference Thompson (1967).
49 Nicholas Kitchen, New England Conservatory of Music blog post (July 27, 2011), http://necmusic.wordpress.com/2011/07/27/guest-bloggers-quartetutopia-by-nicholas-kitchen/ (last accessed January 20, 2015).

distractions or, worse, mutinies against Dubinsky's competence and authority.[50]

In actual practice, a string quartet's sound will likely exhibit features of both styles, depending on the requirements of the music being interpreted. David Soyer, cellist of the Guarneri Quartet, widely regarded during its forty-five year career (1964–2009) as a quintessentially "American" ensemble in terms of both nationality and approach, explains: "The core of the matter is that the unanimity of our approach in a performance is determined not by a preconceived philosophy of what string-quartet playing is supposed to be but by our musical conception of the work at hand. We're four musicians performing a single piece of music, and we come to a common opinion about that work."[51] Guarneri Quartet second violinist John Dalley elaborates: "Each piece will make its own demands; you can't put down a general rule about 'blending.' There are many passages which require a total blend... But sometimes you have the opposite problem: that of blending too well. For instance, certain voices may not stand out in adequate relief."[52] The actual situation at hand and the necessity of "coming to a common opinion" dictate the type of blending that is sought.

Starting with the individual voices—the ideas and opinions of each of the four players—and proceeding by seeking common ground in shaping a unified interpretation, the Guarneri work method is decidedly conversational. It is also liberal because it leaves open the possibility of individual variations in performance within the framework of the established interpretation. Through their conscious interpretative choices—at times made individually, at others as a group— the members of the Guarneri Quartet attempt to balance group unity with member individuality, and to make this balance *audibly apparent* to their listeners.

In my opinion, this liberally oriented work method only really works when it is grounded in a set of unspoken, *unifying communitarian ideals* that govern the quartet as a work group. For me, all members of the ensemble should

---

50 See Rostislav Dubinsky, *Stormy Applause: Making Music in a Worker's State* (New York: Hill and Wang, 1989).
51 Quoted in David Blum and Guarneri Quartet, *The Art of Quartet Playing: The Guarneri Quartet in Conversation with David Blum* (Ithaca: Cornell University Press, 1986), 4.
52 Quoted in ibid., 4.

- come from a similar professional background, with similar training in a specific set of skills;
- be rooted in the same tradition of music as a social practice;
- have similar reasons for being members of the ensemble, and have all voluntarily chosen to become members;
- have a similar awareness and transcendence of the drawbacks of this type of work (long hours, unstable compensation, psychological drain, etc.);
- have a commitment to the same goals of high performance standards, faithfulness to the composer's intentions, etc.;
- have the ability and the inner need to "listen and respond to each other"—to embrace the reciprocal interdependence so intrinsic to chamber music rehearsal and performance.

I believe that the greater the extent to which each of these ideals is realized within the group, the greater the chances of satisfactorily modeling and exemplifying ideal relationships through the social practice of string quartet playing.

Quartet Playing Styles of the Dimov and Sofia Quartets

For twelve seasons I performed internationally as the cellist of the Sofia Quartet, a resident chamber ensemble of the Sofia Philharmonic Orchestra. Prior to that I was a member of the Dimov Quartet for five seasons. My experiences in these two chamber ensembles illustrate the relations among specific groups of people united in a common social practice, in which the participants are assumed to share the same understanding of the "unifying communitarian ideals" outlined above, but in fact have internally conflicted and externally conflicting individual interests.

Dimov Quartet. The Dimov Quartet was founded in 1956 by its first violinist Prof. Dimo Dimov. While the other members of the quartet have changed over the years, Prof. Dimov was the ensemble's constant, its unbroken connection to its own traditions. When I joined the quartet in 1997, I replaced its first non-Bulgarian member, the Russian cellist Nikolai Bespalov, who had decided to emigrate to Germany for greater job security and financial reward. At the time, the other members joked that replacing their Russian member with an American one was a clever political realignment. They also hinted at the possible benefits that I might bring to the group—concerts sponsored by the U. S. Embassy, North American concert tours, recording contracts with U. S. labels, etc. Already there was a rift between my musical reasons for joining the quartet and my colleagues' non-musical reasons for welcoming me as a new member, a rift rooted in individual (mis)understandings of what it is to be "American." I saw myself as an adventurous musician seeking a rewarding "conversation" with like-minded colleagues in a foreign country. To my colleagues, I was an American, and therefore financially well off and professionally well-connected. Any musical qualities I might bring to the table were relatively unimportant. And as the youngest member of a group whose first violinist, at sixty, was exactly twice my age, my own expectations for convergent points of view, for a "conversation among equals," were naively misguided.

The Dimov Quartet, in this incarnation with myself as cellist, was decidedly "European" both in terms of the sound ideal that was sought and the means that were used to achieve it. While trying to appear open to discussion, Prof. Dimov more than once admitted that he had "already had all those arguments" about interpretation (he and the quartet's original cellist, Dimiter Kozev, are said to have argued constantly in rehearsals). He preferred to tell the rest of us how the music should go and became impatient when anyone disagreed. He occasionally indirectly praised me for not challenging his authority. ("Why can't you be like Geoff and just say "dobre" ["okay"] and do it my way?" was his question to the violist in one particularly heated rehearsal.) Like Dubinsky in the original Borodin Quartet, Dimov was by unspoken assent the artistic director of the quartet, deciding what, where, when, and *how* we would perform. To me this seemed an acceptable compromise, since Dimov was clearly the most experienced member of the group.

Dimov's ideal quartet sound—homogenous and completely blended—was typically European. I believe that the many recordings the original Dimov Quartet made for Harmonia mundi and Balkanton in the 1960s, and the intense daily rehearsal routine of those early years, had a major influence on what he perceived as ideal. His concept of blending seemed foreign to the realities of the concert hall, of an acoustic environment that the performers can confront and work with, but cannot control or alter. He never wanted any one voice within the quartet to stand out from the whole, and he spent much time in our rehearsals bringing the general dynamic level down. He routinely chastised us for basically being ourselves, criticizing the second violinist for trying to project his own line in the music and the violist for his habit of "swelling" on long held notes instead of keeping an even dynamic level. When he felt he needed to discourage what he perceived as my own ambitions to be heard above the others, he would just look across at me (we used the European seating arrangement), smile knowingly, and slowly lower his left hand, palm down, in a "shushing" gesture.

Sofia Quartet. The Sofia Quartet, whose members from 2002 through 2014 had, with the exception of the first violinist, been together in the 1997–2002 version of the Dimov Quartet, in some ways cultivated an American approach to an extreme. This was perhaps in part due to our mutual desire to allow our individualities free reign following the period of Dimov-directed "repression," but also to a general unwillingness to commit to the kind of painstaking rehearsals that each of us knew deep down is necessary to achieve a mutually satisfactory group sound. The major criticism from other musicians of our local performances at Bulgaria Hall and the National Palace of Culture was usually that we "didn't sound like a quartet," but rather like four soloists who have come together by chance and seem to have no real desire to conform to or be limited by each other's ideas of how the music should be interpreted.

On occasion, the spark caught fire in performance, and we proved that we did have the ability to "listen and respond to each other" and could apply that ability—if we felt like it. Among our members there was a variance in the intensity of the inner *need* to listen and respond. The listening/responding capability was tempered, or thwarted, by lack of desire. Instead of four equals in conversation, the musical result at times was of four equals engaging in simultaneous monologues and trying not to be distracted by the others. At these times, as the Guarneri Quartet's Michael Tree puts it, the performance would sound as if we were "arguing."[53]

This argumentative quality is the result of the mutual unwillingness of two or more of the members to step back and let another line in the music be heard above his own. In such moments, interpersonal relations among the players are allowed to take primacy over the requirements of the music itself, and the music is simply used as a means of "being heard" or "asserting oneself on stage." The performance ceases to be an interpretative act because players whose interpretative disagreements have not been resolved through a disciplined rehearsal process essentially "play out" their lingering differences on stage.

Early on I asserted my Americanness by insisting on the standard American-style seating arrangement, with the cellist sitting between the second violinist and the violist rather than across from the first violinist

---

53   Quoted in ibid., 6.

(the standard European-style arrangement). I did this more as a symbol of change than from any conviction that a quartet sounds better in the American configuration. Later I decided that the European arrangement is more logical for certain repertoire and wanted to move back to the outside, but our second violinist dissuaded me because he and the violist were not getting along!

The one member of any string quartet whose position never physically changes, no matter what seating arrangement is employed, is the first violinist. His position on the outside left is the equivalent to the placement of the concertmaster, the leader of the first violins of the orchestra. The concertmaster position is a prestigious one of high responsibility and correspondingly high remuneration. When a soloist performs with an orchestra, the first violins move back so that the position of the soloist is roughly where the concertmaster normally is, so this position carries with it certain embedded perceptions of "standing out" from the group in which one is a member, for the player and audience members alike. The concertmaster is perceived as a leader whom others must follow in the service of a common good, that of preserving the "spirit of the music." The soloist's role is similarly a leadership one, but his technically demanding solo part rarely "blends" with the orchestra—this part is intended to project above the orchestra, which provides a subsidiary accompaniment.

In my observation, the concertmaster/soloist model cannot be transferred "as is" to string quartet playing. If the first violinist is unwilling to relinquish at least to some degree his individual sovereignty, to reciprocate the interdependence of the other members of the group by seeing himself as "one of them," it significantly reduces the chances of success for the chamber music project. The first violinist of the Sofia Quartet from 2002 to 2014 was a former concertmaster whose approach to chamber music revealed an internal conflict between "standing out and being heard" and being an equal—but not privileged—partner in the music-making. To his credit, he approached chamber music with the best of intentions and attempted to ignore or transcend any cognitive dissonance he might have had about his place in the ensemble.

In the end I think it comes back to the balance between Small's musicking relationships. If we unconsciously emphasize the unhealthy or poorly developed relationships among the players, we manipulate the music rather than expressing it in a natural way that lets the music "speak for itself." Instead of hearing music and the ideal relationships it embodies, our listeners hear *us* and the distorted relationships embodied in musical interpretations based at least in part on our refusal to interact for the common good. In my opinion, this refusal stems in part I from a fear that if we did dedicate ourselves to developing the "natural" relationships inherent in the music, we might in the long run have proven unable to *sustain* the same level of commitment or meet the accordingly heightened expectations of our audiences and colleagues. Consistent averageness somehow seemed more desirable than inconsistent greatness. The result of this refusal seems to demonstrate the damage to the group caused when individual interests are not aligned with or not allowed to be subsumed by group interests, when the members are not attuned to each other's needs or to the fact that they, each and all, belong to a common tradition of social practice.

My experiences in the Dimov and Sofia Quartets have given me some of the high points in my professional career as a performing musician. They have also shown me both the necessity of finding an adequate balance of liberal and communitarian thinking and action, and the enormous difficulty of actually achieving this balance. The best professional quartets are said to recognize certain paradoxes and to transcend them without actually talking about them.[54] We didn't talk about them either, but if we had, the responses would likely have highlighted the striking divergence of individual interests and motivations within the group.

---

54 Murnighan and Conlon, "The Dynamics of Intense Work Groups," 177-178.

Chapter 6

The Ethics of Entrainment: Music-Making and Habermasian Practical Discourse

What role might the activity of making music together have in the actualization of Jürgen Habermas' discourse ethics? In this chapter I attempt to show that participatory artistic experience creates conditions under which practical discourse is more likely to take place. Entrainment, a universal human trait that privileges temporal regularity, facilitates the mutual reciprocity identified in Chapter 5 as a crucial component of interactive music-making. The situational and developmental functions of music in enabling social and intellectual flexibility can be seen as "preconditions for the emergence of abstract concepts that frame and give meaning to human interaction, such as that of social justice..."[1] Habermas himself acknowledges the place of aesthetic thinking in his "unity of reason,"[2] and recognizes the potential of art to address "questions of motivation" in ethics of justice.[3]

While reasoning is certainly central to a deliberative process that is to result in mutual understanding, human concern for fairness and equity in the treatment of groups of people requires both a motivational ground and a high level of adaptability in our social interactions. As Ian Cross maintains,

> Human musicality appears to provide co-ordinative and open frameworks for interaction, maintaining and perhaps forming the intellectual and social flexibility that is manifested in our capacity for shared intentionality. Musicality does not give rise to social justice, but at an evolutionary timescale it is likely that it has provided space for the emergence of concepts that bear on how humans can, and ultimately perhaps should, interact.[4]

---

1   Ian Cross, "Music and Social Being," *Musicology Australia*, Vol. 28, no. 1 (2005): 123.
2   Jürgen Habermas, *Moral Consciousness and Communicative Action*, trans. C. Lenhardt and S. W. Nicolsen (Cambridge: MIT Press, 1990), 17.
3   Jürgen Habermas, *Justification and Application*, trans. C. Cronin (Cambridge: MIT Press, 1993), 75.
4   Cross, "Music and Social Being," 124.

In what follows I argue that the participatory music-making situation can be construed both as a *prelude* to the practical discourse of Habermas' discourse ethics and as a *model* for the prosocial interaction that such discourse requires.

Habermas' Unity of Reason and Discourse Ethics

In assessing the current state of philosophy and proposing a way forward in *Moral Consciousness and Communicative Action*, Habermas argues for a reunification of reason. He wants philosophy to be able to relinquish its supposed role—as implied by Kant and Hegel—of "supreme judge…in matters of science as well as culture" *without* giving up its status as "the guardian of rationality." Similarly to the totality of science, the totality of culture and its rational structures—or its "cultural value spheres," after Max Weber and Emil Lask—need in Habermas' view to be described and analyzed rather than philosophically justified or grounded.[5]

According to Habermas, the reunification of reason must properly take place at the level of "everyday communication": "reaching understanding in the lifeworld requires a cultural tradition that ranges across *the whole spectrum*, not just the fruits of science and technology." Acting as a mediating "interpreter on behalf of the lifeworld," philosophy could then remobilize the "interplay between the cognitive-instrumental, moral-practical, and aesthetic-expressive dimensions," corresponding to the three isolated aspects of rationality: science, morals, and art.[6]

Habermas asserts that "pragmatism and hermeneutics have joined forces… [in] attributing epistemic authority to the community of those who cooperate and speak with one another." Action that has mutual understanding as its goal already has unconditionality embedded in its structure, offering evidence that agreements are based on grounds and therefore making "the validity (*Gultigkeit*) that we claim for our views different from the mere de facto acceptance (*Geltung*) of habitual practices." For Habermas, social practices of justification are therefore something more than *just* social practices: they have a rational grounding of which philosophy is the guardian.[7]

In arguing that everyday life is the medium that will allow reason to continue as "a unity on the level of culture," Habermas looks to artistic

---

5 Habermas, *Moral Consciousness and Communicative Action*, 16–17.
6 Ibid., 18–19; Habermas' emphasis.
7 Ibid., 18–19.

counter-movements such as postmodern art. In the realm of art—the aspect of rationality dealing with taste—the trend toward autonomous art has led it "to mirror one basic aesthetic experience, the increasing decentration of subjectivity...as the subject leaves the spatiotemporal structures of everyday life behind, freeing itself from the conventions of everyday perception, of purposive behavior, and of the imperatives of work and utility." In postmodern art, seemingly against all probability, "realistic, politically committed schools" coexist with the equally sincere adherents of classical modernism. Habermas finds that in the art of the politically committed schools, "elements of the cognitive and the moral-practical come into play once again...[in] the wealth of forms unloosed by the avant-garde," in effect implementing a reunification of reason.[8] I will return to Habermas' views on aesthetics shortly.

Habermas' vision of the workings of unity of reason through communicative action is articulated in his Discourse Ethics. Habermas' cognitivist theory is enabled by **practical discourse** delineated by its publicly enacted intersubjective impartiality. It will soon become apparent how the fundamental characteristics of Habermasian Discourse Ethics are also central to the activity of making music.

The Governing Principle (U). Habermas characterizes his view "that normative rightness must be regarded as a claim to validity that is analogous to a truth claim" as **cognitivist ethics**, which "must answer the question of how to justify normative statements." Discourse ethics offers a procedure of moral argumentation that reduces the Kantian categorical imperative to a universal principle (U). This governing principle of discourse ethics states: "Only those norms may claim to be valid that could meet with the consent of all affected in their role as participants in a practical discourse."[9]

Universal Validity. Habermas defends his position that discourse ethics is a **universalist ethics** by arguing that it overcomes what might be termed the "ethnocentric fallacy." He asserts that its moral principle (U), "far from reflecting the intuitions of a particular culture or epoch, is valid universally... Anyone who seriously undertakes to participate in argumentation implicitly accepts by that very undertaking general pragmatic presuppositions that have a normative content."[10]

---

8   Ibid., 17–18.
9   Ibid., 197.
10 Ibid., 197–8.

Impartial Judgment. The practical discourse of Habermas' theory is also governed by (U), which also functions as a rule of argumentation guiding a "cooperative search for truth, where nothing coerces anyone except the force of the better argument." It facilitates the attainment of a moral point of view, "from which moral questions can be judged *impartially.*" The Habermasian procedure of practical discourse contrasts with formalist theories such as that of John Rawls, whose original position veil of ignorance Habermas rejects as unnecessary. As an exacting form of argumentative decision making, practical discourse establishes the rightness or fairness of a normative agreement reached through free participatory argumentation by allowing for the "idealized, partly counterfactual presuppositions…that participants in argumentation do in fact make."[11]

Public and Intersubjective. Habermas' practical discourse is fully **participatory**, and its impartiality is guaranteed **intersubjectively** through reciprocal perspective-taking. While Mead's formalist theory of ideal role-taking in order to understand how affected parties would be impacted by a proposed plan or new norm envisions it as individual and privately enacted, practical discourse transforms role-taking "into a *public* affair, practiced intersubjectively by all involved."[12]

Mutual Perspective-taking. Perspective-taking is central to Habermas' thought, and he devotes much space to elucidating his position on it. He situates Kolhberg's perspectives within interlocking systems of world and speaker perspectives that are the foundation of Habermas' theory of communicative action both suggested by and necessary to his discourse ethics. Like Kohlberg, Habermas approaches these perspectives developmentally. He then reconstructs them as "stages of interaction" that progressively decenter how a child understands the world, establishing that "the nexus between conceptions of the world and claims to validity opens the possibility of linking the reflective attitude toward the social world…with the hypothetical attitude of a participant in argumentation." This process leads from reflectivity to reflexivity, from which the moral point of view develops in discourse ethics.[13]

Habermas discusses three different world perspectives, asserting that for an intelligible spoken utterance to be accepted as valid, it must meet one of three criteria: it either represents states of affairs in *the* world (the truth criteria), maintains an interpersonal relationship in *our* world (the

---

11   Ibid., 198; Habermas' emphasis.
12   Ibid., 197–8; Habermas' emphasis.
13   Ibid., 130–2.

rightness criteria), or manifests lived experience in *each participant's own world* (the truthfulness criteria).[14] He then elaborates on his conception of a developmentally-progressive system of speaker perspectives. One of the important features of this system is that the perspectives are "fully reversible."[15]

Habermas here follows Selman, tracing three levels of speaker-perspective development: *Level 1,* with **differentiated and subjective perspective-taking** where, according to Selman, "relating of perspectives is conceived of in one-way, unilateral terms"; *Level 2,* with **self-reflective/second-person and reciprocal perspective-taking,** where reciprocity takes the form of "two single individuals seeing self and other, but not the relationship system between them"; and *Level 3,* where individuals have both the ability and the intellectual need to engage in **coordinated mutual perspective-taking,** because they have come to the understanding that only through coordination can positive social outcomes be achieved. Relations at Level 3 are seen by the those engaged in them "as ongoing systems in which thoughts and experiences are mutually shared."[16]

The Care-Free Empathy of Mutual Perspective-Taking

In his introduction to Habermas' *Moral Consciousness and Communicative Action,* Thomas McCarthy asserts that "Habermas' discourse model...builds the moment of empathy *into* the procedure of coming to a reasoned agreement."[17] This statement is problematic because Habermas' own understanding of empathy is such that the construct is of little use to him for three main reasons. First, Habermas sees empathy as a one-sided activity as opposed to the mutually reciprocal perspective-taking that his discourse ethics requires. Second, he considers as definitive Gadamer's hermeneutic critique of empathy: because we are culturally embedded, we cannot bracket our own background and hermeneutic perspective.[18] As Habermas elaborates elsewhere, "the layer of traditions in which identities are formed" and "an individual's or a group's historically changing interpretations of the world and of themselves" must be considered. Habermas

---

14   Ibid., 137–38.
15   Ibid., 142.
16   Selman quoted in ibid., 142–44.
17   McCarthy in ibid., viii; McCarthy's emphasis.
18   Ibid., 28.

overturns Kant's assumption that moral judgments can be justifiably arrived at by an individual who simply projects himself

> into the situation of everyone else through his own imagination. [Because] the participants can no longer rely on a transcendental preunderstanding grounded in more or less homogeneous conditions of life and interests, the moral point of view can only be realized under conditions of communication that ensure that everyone tests the acceptability of a norm, implemented in a general practice, also from the perspective of his own understanding of himself and of the world...[19]

Third, because Habermas accepts that empathy comprises both affective and cognitive aspects, its caring component, were it to be allowed in Habermas' theory, would clash with justice as a moral point of view. The partiality implied by acts of caring conflicts with the "purely cognitive and impartial ideal role-taking procedures of moral judgment."[20] Rather than trying to bracket the caring component of empathy as others[21] have attempted to do, Habermas opts instead to think in terms of **mutual perspective-taking**.

A recurring criticism of Habermas' strict rational application of "universal norms to adjudicate between competing value convictions" is that its "strict delineation between affective, asymmetrical attachments of ethical care and the impartial, symmetrical relations of moral justice undercuts the motivation of moral agents to engage in the public contestation of competing value claims."[22] Indeed Habermas himself criticizes Kohlberg's version of ideal perspective-taking precisely because it incorporates both affective and cognitive features into the process. Vetlesen offers the following account of the differences between the Habermas and Kohlberg perspective-taking theories:

> whereas Kohlberg depicts the ascendance from context-specific to universal role taking as having throughout the form of a joint undertaking of our cognitive and emotional faculties (in which we cognitively reach a higher level of reflexivity and abstraction, and in which we emotionally move from simple identification through diffuse empathy toward sympathy as the recognition of the integrity and uniqueness

---

19 Jürgen Habermas, "Communicative Ethics," in *The Inclusion of the Other. Studies in Political Theory* (Cambridge: MIT Press, 1998).
20 Habermas quoted in Richard Ganis, *The Politics of Care in Habermas and Derrida: Between Measurability and Immeasurability* (Lanham: Rowman and Littlefield, 2011), 26.
21 Cf. Alvin I. Goldman, 2006.
22 Jeffrey Epstein, review of Richard Ganis, *The Politics of Care in Habermas and Derrida*, in Plurilogue: Politics and Philosophy Reviews, no. 11 (2012). http://www.plurilogue.com/2012/11/the-politics-of-care-in-habermas-and.html (last accessed January 24, 2015).

of alter), Habermas admits our emotional faculty only at the start of this movement ... The role of emotions is restricted to the initial opening up of the moral phenomena to be discussed from a hypothetical point of view, discussion here meaning the purely cognitive redeeming of the validity claim of normative rightness.[23]

In an apparent rejection of caring and emotional impact as necessary features of perspective-taking and therefore of attaining a moral point of view, Habermas argues against Kohlberg that respect and caring are not intrinsic to empathy. He also points out that Kohlberg's principle of equal respect applies only to individuals, not to caring about larger, generalized groups of people, and that Kohlberg fails to show an unequivocal link between justice and good will.[24]

Without referencing Habermas directly, two articles by Paul Bloom offer insights supporting Habermas' arguments against affective empathy. While several scholarly authors had joined President Obama's call for "an increase in empathy as a cure for humanity's ills," Bloom challenges their enthusiasm for empathy, taking what I would characterize as a rational Habermasian stance in arguing against the usefulness of empathy in public deliberation. He asserts that the empathy—understood here in terms of its affective connotation as the compassionate caring that stems from placing oneself imaginatively in someone else's situation and identifying with what that person may be thinking or feeling—we feel for single victims whose images, names, and stories are shared overrides our willingness to act to help much larger numbers of nameless victims. Too often the identifiable victim is the victim that we have been manipulated through media or other public attention to empathize with.[25]

Highlighting a particularly alarming instance of the kind of irrational response that empathy as caring can engender, particularly if we "take it as a moral guide," Bloom reports that certain segments of the population are feeling compassion toward the young man whose bombs had killed several people and maimed many more during the Boston Marathon. The "warmth and compassion directed toward [Dzhokhar] Tsarnaev by certain teen-age girls and, weirdly, by *mothers*" may have stemmed from the initial description of Tsarnaev as "a hapless genial pothead being coerced into killing by his sadistic older brother. But [Hanna Rosin] later settles on

---

23 Arne Johan Vetlesen, *Perception, Empathy, and Judgment: An Inquiry into the Preconditions of Moral Performance* (University Park: Pennsylvania State University Press, 1994), 318.
24 Ibid., 318.
25 Paul Bloom, "The Baby in the Well: The Case Against Empathy," *The New Yorker* (May 20, 2013); Bloom's emphasis.

an account which I believe is both unsettling and correct: "Dzhokhar is cute."" Certain specific combinations of facial features can trigger empathy, while others—such as those of a surly-looking criminal—can discourage it. Tsarnaev was reaping the benefits of not possessing a stereotypical "criminal look," as girls and mothers were literally being blinded by empathy, which prevented them from "seeing" Tsarnaev as a villain. Paradoxically, in identifying *with* him, they failed to identify *him*, simply because they found him attractive.[26]

Bloom contrasts the empathy-influenced short-term fix, where action is taken after a tragedy befalls a person or group, with rationally motivated long-term policies, where action is taken in advance to prevent such things from happening to even larger groups of people. One of the specific examples he gives concerns global warming, then a "heated" subject of debate in the U. S. Congress: "the limits of empathy are especially stark here. Opponents of restrictions on CO_2 emissions are flush with identifiable victims—all those who will be harmed by increased costs, by business closures. The millions of people who at some unspecified future date will suffer the consequences of our current inaction are, by contrast, pale statistical abstractions." Bloom's cognitivist conclusion is that the future welfare of the billions of potential victims inhibiting the planet demands "deliberation and calculation," because a "reasoned, even counter-empathetic analysis of moral obligation and likely consequences is a better guide to planning for the future than the gut wrench of empathy." He is not suggesting we should avoid empathizing; he is simply warning against allowing affective empathy to *solely* dictate our decision-making, lead us into action, or guide our public policy-making.[27]

Some scholars strenuously maintain that affective caring needs to be integrated into Habermasian thought. Ganis argues that "the requirements of deontological, universalistic moral theory constrain him [Habermas] from fully bridging the conceptual gulf between the two standpoints"—care and justice—and calls for a revision of Habermas' discourse ethics that more adequately incorporates affective attachments of care.[28] Others insist on revising existing models of empathy to make them serviceable in the realm of deliberative action. For example, Morrell has modified Davis'

---

26 Paul Bloom, "Feeling Sorry for Tsarnaev," *The New Yorker* blog (May 16, 2013), http://www.newyorker.com/news/news-desk/feeling-sorry-for-tsarnaev (last accessed January 22, 2015). Bloom references Hanna Rosin, "Why All This Maternal Sympathy for Dzhokhar?" (April 29, 2013), https:slate.com (last accessed January 22, 2015).
27 Paul Bloom, "The Baby in the Well."
28 Richard Ganis, *The Politics of Care in Habermas and Derrida*, 37.

conception of empathy to achieve "a model of empathy as a process, rather than a state, that...accounts for the various conceptualizations of empathy[,] integrates affect and cognition, [and] also explains the relationship between empathy and sympathy, two concepts theorists often use interchangeably."[29]

The Music-Making Situation as an Ethical Model

Habermas himself relates both aesthetic and therapeutic criticism, where rationally motivated agreement is not a requirement, to forms of argumentation that together with theoretical, explicative, and practical discourse make up a system of argumentation. He sees the existence of forms of argumentation with "more lenient criteria" as a liability for practical discourse, a liability stemming from "the sociohistorical situatedness of reason."[30] He seems to be suggesting that the effectiveness of practical discourse reaches its limit or is diminished when it must contend with forms of argumentation where reason is not rigorously applied.

But does aesthetic thinking set a limit for reason, or does it in fact push that limit aside? By treating art as subjective affective expression, Habermas seems to perpetuate the old fallacy of isolating art from the everyday lifeworld in which he situates the public intersubjective interactions of practical discourse. Boucher finds in Habermas' formulation of a distinct aesthetic dimension of communicative reason a proposal that "artworks are not primarily "ways of seeing," that is, vehicles for truth claims modelled on cognitive truth, but feeling complexes, whose truthfulness involves a distinct sort of non-cognitive—but certainly not irrational—claim." In fulfilling responsibility for "the experimental expression of human needs...artworks provide the motivational structures necessary for moral autonomy and scientific thinking."[31]

If artistic experience is looked upon as a social practice—as an intersubjective activity in which the participants are fully engaged—its potential significance to discourse ethics significantly expands. First, participatory artistic experience creates conditions under which practical discourse can take place. Further, as Czobor-Lupp argues, the "aesthetic

---

29 Michael E. Morrell, *Empathy and Democracy: Feeling, Thinking, and Deliberation* (University Park: Pennsylvania State University Press, 2010), 14.
30 Habermas, *Moral Consciousness and Communicative Action*, 105–6.
31 Geoff Boucher, "The Politics of Aesthetic Affect—A Reconstruction of Habermas' Art Theory," *Parrhesia*, no. 13 (2011): 62–63.

dimension" of the dialogue ensures that dialogue continues, even when agreement is not possible. She identifies an

> incipient thread in Habermas' discourse ethics that recognizes the importance of linguistic creativity and of imagination in communicative practice. ...Even when rational consensus and agreement cannot be achieved, dialogue is still not abandoned. This is the case because, through a larger definition of the dialogical, which adds to the discursive aspect, an aesthetic, rhetorical, and metaphorical dimension, it is possible to say that, even when conflicting, different voices and languages are still creatively and imaginatively interilluminating and hybridizing each other. Thus, they still transform each other, creating, at the same time, a prediscursive commonality, that can function as a necessary prerequisite for intercultural understanding.[32]

I believe that this "prediscursive commonality" is at the basis of Habermas' "shared lifeworld" and becomes apparent during the processes of social interaction exemplified by the music-making situation. The aesthetic dimension has a role precisely in *situations* where commonality becomes recognizable. It is the aesthetic dimension of our experience that encourages our very openness to the *possibility* of dialogue and the understandings it can potentially produce. In my view, the prediscursive element does not simply imply that our receptiveness to our commonality precedes argumentative discourse, but also that it can precede *any* use of language as a communicative tool. The participatory music-making situation is also prediscursive because it starts from *perceived* shared understanding. This perception may or may not be accurate, but the fact that it is mutually reciprocated among the participants leads to a positive, satisfying music-making experience, which in turn heightens the desirability of the perception and offers a rational basis for taking the perception to be true.

At the level of language use, this receptivity to the possibility of dialogue is seen in the way we use culturally pervasive patterned statements at the opening of a conversation, not to exchange any important information, but simply to keep alive the potential for further interaction. In his research with primitive cultures, Bronisław Malinowski observes what he terms *phatic communion*.[33] Characteristic of the phatic dimension of communication is that at this stage in the dialogue any responses beyond the culturally-established "stock" replies to questions such as "How are you?"

---

[32] Mihaela Czobor-Lupp, "Communicative Reason and Intercultural Understanding: A Critical Discussion of Habermas," *European Journal of Political Theory*, 7 (2008): 430.

[33] Bronisław Malinowski, "The problem of meaning in primitive languages," in Supplement I to C. K. Ogden and I. A. Richards, *The Meaning of Meaning: A Study of the Influence of Language upon Thought and of the Science of Symbolism*, (Cambridge: University of Cambridge, 1923), 296–336.

are seen as inappropriate because they break unwritten social rules. These pre-understood rules govern the phatic level of interaction in what Cross refers to as "situations of social uncertainty," where the subsequent course and outcome of the situation are unknown to the participants and the interaction is designed to leave all options open.[34]

Cross' research suggests that both music and language can be considered modes of communication and appear to share some of the same resources. However, he makes four important distinctions between these two "context-specific manifestations of a common substrate for human communicative capacities":

> Language and music can be distinguished semantically in terms of their capacity to embody articulate propositions, ... structurally in terms of the extent to which affective/rhythmic or syntactical/semantic features are foregrounded... [and] in terms of the communicative contexts within which they tend to be efficaciously deployed. Language can be thought of as mobilizing shared intentionality for goal-directed behavior, while music can be interpreted as mobilizing shared intentionality per se.[35]

Cross maintains that the social practice of music-making as a participatory group activity surpasses language use in its potential for effectively managing situations of social uncertainty because the possibility of misinterpreting referential meaning, ever-present in speech communication, is absent in music. This makes music an ideal communicative mode for non-conflictual group interaction. Since musical meaning is non-referential, music can be experienced as if it is an "honest symbol" of unmediated meaning. In Cross' view, music is experienced through a floating intentionality in which an individual's private meanings are not required to be made known to other participants. Because the experience is being shared through the sharing of time together, it leads to bonding among the participants, and the participants are free—and more likely—to imagine that each of the other participants is thinking and feeling the same way about the experience.[36] Elsewhere Cross elaborates on his vision of the intersubjective nature of participatory music-making:

> Music's floating intentionality allows participants to interpret a flow of musical behaviors and sounds in individual terms while the temporal regularities of the framework that it provides act to co-ordinate their behaviors and attentional foci...

---

34 Ian Cross, "Music, speech and meaning in interaction," keynote address, 12th International Congress on Musical Signification, Louvain-la-Neuve, Belgium, April 2, 2013.
35 Ian Cross, "Music as a social and cognitive process," in *Language and Music as Cognitive Systems*, ed. P. Rebuschat et al. (London: Oxford University Press, 2011).
36 Cross, "Music, speech and meaning in interaction."

> Hence participants in a collective musical act—and I include both dance and ostensibly passive listening in this category—may each experience that musical act as bearing personal and potentially quite different, though determinate, significances without the integrity of the collective musical act being undermined.[37]

The "temporal regularities" of the musical framework suggest a kind of rule that governs the activity. The mutual coordination of musical interactions among the participants, known as *entrainment,* is "based on the abstraction of a regular periodic pulse from sequences of rhythmic events and the organization of the timing of actions and sounds around the abstracted pulse." Entrainment is possible because of our "tendency to privilege information that occurs at regular temporal intervals." As a significant example of "the influence of our common perceptual and cognitive endowment on musical practice," entrainment emerges as a human ability that is not culturally specific, but is in fact a universal human endowment.[38]

Music also possesses a functional universality. The "profound functional commonality in music across cultures" has its basis in music's essential ambiguity of meaning. Music "is rarely used in any society for only one purpose but tends to manifest itself in a wide range of contexts where meanings are open, where the boundaries of permissible behavior are not clearly or explicitly delineated (though it will typically be oriented around a shared timeframe for all participants)." Music's floating intentionality "guarantee[s] the success of social interaction by creating conditions for the minimization of conflict through its semantic open-ness while simultaneously enabling a joint sense of shared action that is oriented around commonly experienced temporal regularities." This openness can be contrasted with the restrictions imposed by language when it is the medium of interaction. Language's referential essence limits how an individual interprets any given linguistic behavior, and its potential for being used manipulatively limits the possibilities for interpreting what role each participant plays in the interaction.[39] The participatory music-making situation anticipates the last of Kohlberg's six sociomoral perspectives referred to by Habermas. According to Kohlberg, this stage "takes the perspective of a moral point of view from which social arrangements

---

37 Cross, "Music and Social Being," 122.
38 Ibid., 118.
39 Ibid., 121–2.

derive or on which they are grounded [, with] the basic moral premise of respect for other persons as ends, not means."[40]

I propose that the music-making situation can be conceived of in terms of Habermas' "action situation and speech situation." Habermas defines a situation as "a segment of a lifeworld that has been delimited in terms of a specific theme." Broadly stated, the theme of the music-making situation, in accordance with the interests and objectives of the participants, is the music to be made. The activity of making music (the action situation) involves the taking of communicative roles as described by Habermas: "to these roles correspond first- and second-person *participant perspectives* as well as the third-person *observer perspective* from which the I-thou relation is observed as an intersubjective complex and can thus be objectified."[41] Musical sound replaces speech as the mode of communication, so if "communicative" is used in place of "speech," the music-making situation appears to meet Habermas' criteria for being simultaneously an action situation and a communicative situation.

Habermas' explanation of the lifeworld as both a common context and a provider of shared resources for the participants in communicative action also seems to be applicable to the music-making situation.

> The shared lifeworld offers a storehouse of unquestioned cultural givens from which those participating in communication draw agreed-upon patterns of interpretation for use in their interpretative efforts... The solidarity of groups integrated through values and the competences of socialized individuals also serve as resources for action oriented toward reaching understanding, although in a different way than cultural traditions.[42]

The presuppositions embodied in the shared lifeworld —Habermas' "intuitively preunderstood context"—are on a meta level the "prediscursive commonality" modeled and enhanced by the music-making situation.

Habermas also places the process of achieving understanding on a meta level, as the mediator between the objective world and the subjective lifeworld. Is music a cultural tradition, and therefore part of the preunderstood context for the music-making situation, or is it the "something in the world" about which the participants in communicative action must reach mutual understanding before they implement action plans based on a given

---

40 Lawrence Kohlberg, *Essays on Moral Development, Vol. I: The Philosophy of Moral Development* (San Francisco: Harper and Row, 1981), quoted in Habermas, *Moral Consciousness and Communicative Action*, 129.
41 Habermas, *Moral Consciousness and Communicative Action*, 134–5; Habermas' emphasis.
42 Ibid., 135–6.

action situation? Insofar as a specific music-making situation can be construed as a situation of social uncertainty, the question arises as to what extent that situation can or should be pre-defined by its participants. The unpredictable ways that the situation itself develops, through the interactions of the participants and governed by floating intentionally, seem to preclude pre-definition to some degree.

Because it is grounded in a universal human tendency to privilege temporal regularity, as expressed in the mutual coordination of entrainment, the participatory music-making situation can operate across cultures to rehearse mutual understanding among individuals coming from otherwise divergent cultural contexts. While the intentionality of music-making is shared, it is not fixed, so the very *act* of sharing is more central than *what* is being shared. Due to music's well-documented ability to evoke emotions, the sharing in musical experience may be considered both cognitive and affective: it has both sharing and caring connotations. Habermas himself acknowledges affective caring or concern for others as a motivator of practical discourse and the mutual understanding it seeks.

The existence of participatory music-making in cultures throughout the world marks it as a universal norm. As something that people often do together and have done for generations, it represents a cultural value. Habermas characterizes cultural values as "components of intersubjectively shared traditions."[43] As such the music-making situation both precedes and enables the practical discourse at the heart of Habermas' discourse ethics, and embodies its main features. Music-making is

- ***Public.*** It brings people together in public space;
- ***Intersubjective.*** It facilitates the desire for and enactment of mutual affiliation, heightening the perception of mutually reciprocal thoughts and feelings embodied in the experience;
- ***Cognitive.*** This perception is itself a cognitive process;
- ***Universal.*** It reflects cultural practice in otherwise diverse cultures, supporting Habermas' claim of universality for participatory discourse as a means of achieving agreement on validity claims.

The participatory music-making situation can be construed both as a prelude to the practical discourse of Habermas' discourse ethics and as a model for the prosocial interaction that such discourse requires. For

---

43   Ibid., 67–68.

specific examples I now turn to several group music projects I have initiated as artistic director of the AmBul Festival of American and Bulgarian Music and projects director of the Ardenza Foundation, both based in Sofia, Bulgaria.

Prosocial Interaction in Music Improvisation Projects

From 2007 I became increasingly involved in musical performance projects that bring together groups of musicians from diverse backgrounds, locations, and generations, often representing differing musical styles.[44] At first the main point of this type of sociomusical experiment was simply to see what would happen when musicians who had never shared the stage before—and probably would never have thought of doing so—were presented with an entirely new performance situation. With little or no rehearsal time before the performance itself, these surprise collaborations became studies in the non-verbal establishment of mutual affinity through shared, public music-making situations.

In C. The first such project was the 2007 Bulgarian premiere of *In C*, a composition by the American composer Terry Riley. First performed in San Francisco in 1964, *In C* is widely regarded as one of the first minimalist compositions. It can be performed by any number of instrumentalists and/or vocalists, and has no set instrumentation (the more players the better) or performance duration (generally around an hour). Each player performs from the same part, consisting of a series of fifty-three melodic figures of differing lengths, to be played in order. The major requirement is that each player repeat each of the figures a different number of times, so that any two players are either overlapping within the same figure or playing different figures simultaneously. Harmonically this works because Riley has carefully planned out the work so that most of it is literally "in C" (in the key of C Major). *In C* is unified by a steady pulse provided by a repeated high C usually played by a keyboard instrument, helping the ensemble stay together rhythmically.

The 2007 performance during the AmBul Festival of American and Bulgarian Music in Sofia featured just six musicians (an unusually small number of players for this work), lasted just half an hour, and was performed in a very small venue (the Boris Christoff Center). Four years later,

---

44 Since the founding of the Ardenza Foundation in 2008 and the reincarnation of American Music Week in Bulgaria (1998–2003) as the AmBul Festival of American and Bulgarian Music.

In C was heard again at AmBul, this time at Studio I of Bulgarian National Radio, again with the Ardenza Trio as the nucleus of the ensemble. This time there were about twenty musicians on stage. The increase in numbers meant that a much wider array of instruments and performer personalities were represented. These included wind and percussion players from the Bourgas National Music School, string players from the National Music Academy in Sofia, and several more experienced professional musicians. The greater numbers also allowed us to expand the performance time of the work to about an hour. At a single rehearsal before the performance, we agreed on several elements that we wanted to achieve in the concert, such as gradual dynamic changes (no dynamics are indicated in the score), unison basses in the middle section were the harmonies turn toward E minor, a trumpet solo near the end highlighting one of the Bourgas musicians, and a kind of wave effect traveling through the ensemble as we created a final fade out. The ensemble was arranged in a large semicircle on stage, with two vocalists placed slightly behind it on the left and two percussionists behind it on the right. The Ardenza Trio was placed at the center of the semicircle.

It is important to emphasize that, as is typical for performances of *In C*, no conductor participated in these concerts. This results in a chamber music type of performance where the performers are listening and reacting to each other rather than simply following a conductor's direction. This also heightens the sense of each musician having an important personal stake in the end result, depending not only on shaping an interpretation, but also on building the composition in real time. As a participant in the 2011 performance, I can say that I have never experienced so intense a level of creative energy and comradery as I felt on stage that evening.

Although I would classify the 2011 performance of *In C* as a successful venture in non-verbal establishment of mutual affinity and consensus, I would not go so far as to suggest that everyone who participated had the same sensations or thoughts about it as I did. Differences in sensation and thinking were *already built into the project* because of the diversity of life and musical experience among the musicians involved. For example, a tenth-grade clarinetist with no previous experience with group improvisation, contemporary music, or this particular work might be more likely to have experienced significant stress in addition to any exhilaration this performance might have brought him. The social experience was vastly different for Sofia-based musicians than for the Bourgas participants, who all knew each other from school, but in most cases had never been to Sofia at all, let alone for a performance at so prestigious venue as Bulgarian National Radio.

Cobra Junior. The *Cobra* gaming pieces by John Zorn use an elaborate system of signals that serves as a framework in performance for experienced improvising musicians. Individually, these performers have clearly delineated musical personalities and repertoires of sounds and instrumental techniques, while as a group they are unified through their similar backgrounds in improvisation and, in many cases, by their familiarity with Mr. Zorn's system. My version moves in the opposite direction, using a simplified signaling system requiring minimal rehearsal to introduce young, inexperienced performers to the possibilities of group interaction through sound. The element of surprise is as pronounced among the performers themselves—who often have no prior experience, even as listeners, to this type of group improvisation—as it is among the audiences at the live performances of the Cobra Junior project. My role as gamemaster is to unify disparate elements and control modes of interaction to create satisfying improvised compositions.

As with *In C*, there is a heightened sense of each performer having a large stake in the creative process, because the form of the resulting composition depends on decisions made on the spur of the moment during the actual performance. As personal choices directly affect the entire group, there is a considerable burden of responsibility attached to them. The Cobra Junior project highlights this responsibility, placing it within the framework of a safe, nonjudgmental context and allowing the performers to hear the consequences of each of their decisions and to participate in redirecting the music when necessary.

One of the trademarks of the Cobra Junior project is the participation of folk musicians alongside colleagues representing classical and jazz playing styles. The jazz musicians tend to approach the project with their own preconceptions about how improvisation is supposed to work, and in some cases actually exhibit *less* flexibility and imagination in unexpected sound situations. They also tend to fall back on certain musical clichés rather than constantly trying to find new sounds. Depending on their stylistic backgrounds, jazz musicians expect an improvised solo to last a certain length of time, often measured in eight or sixteen-bar units to match the duration of the chorus of a jazz standard. The "solos" in *Cobra*, especially in contexts where the musical line cuts rapidly from one player to the next, are often only a second or two long—this can prove creatively frustrating for improvisers who are used to being able to develop their ideas without interruption over a much longer period of performance time.

Any participant in Cobra Junior is more likely to find the experience more rewarding when it is approached from a standpoint of relative ignorance, regardless of one's previous experience in group improvisation. The moment someone decides that they know definitively how the music should develop, or how the interaction among the players should proceed, is the moment the living quality of this type of musical performance dies: because this is a music of *building* relationships rather than merely *exhibiting* pre-existing or potential relationships.

While diversity and individuality are crucial to Cobra Junior on many levels, there are also several communitarian elements at play. There is a set of governing principles or rules, however rudimentary, that guide the modes of interaction among the performers. There is also a gamemaster, a leader of sorts who is charged with interpreting those rules and enforcing them if necessary. A relationship of deep trust in the gamemaster's musical judgment must develop to allow the improvisation to proceed without conflict. In Zorn's original version of *Cobra*, he recognized both the real and theatrical potential of dissenting opinions, and worked in scenarios where players symbolize their disagreement with the gamemaster by donning ninja-like headbands and proceeding to ignore the gamemaster's cues.

In Zorn's version, which has never been officially published and therefore exists in the form of notes compiled and distributed by participants in performances of *Cobra* under Zorn's direction, the gamemaster's visual cues fall into a number of categories and require extensive study or rehearsal time. My version also uses color-coded cue categories, reinforced with colored cards that can be held up, but Zorn's cues also involve combinations of hand shapes and touching different body locations. What is crucial in both versions is constant visual and aural awareness. In the end, as Zorn himself has stated, *Cobra* is not about performers communing with sound—it is about performers communing with each other.

Rila Music Exchange. One of the existing musical forums in Europe that exhibits the features of discourse ethics is the Ethno youth music festival. Such festivals have been organized in various European countries, and a group of Ethno events are held each summer under the auspices of the Brussels-based Jeunesses Musicales International. Ethno festivals tend to have the following characteristics in common:

- Youth (ages 18–30) and musical interest, aptitude, and background;
- All nationalities welcome (ethnic and musical diversity are central to the project);
- Participants live together in a spirit of sharing;
- Participants learn music by ear;
- Participants teach each other;
- Participants work intensively to shape new interpretations and arrangements of songs.

The participants share these new musical arrangements in public performances, and take particular pride in versions that juxtapose songs, cultures, and cross controversial boundaries (e.g., political, or between traditionally warring regions).

Following the Ethno model of youth festival/workshops, the Ardenza Foundation began organizing the annual Rila Music Exchange in 2012. Young people from different backgrounds and countries come together in the town of Rila in early September of each year, spending an intense week teaching each other folk melodies from around the world and collectively preparing new versions of them for a series of outdoor concerts. These village celebrations of music and dance are meetings of tradition and the present-day—of old and young, of Bulgarian and "other"—that transcend cultural and generational differences.

The founding artistic leaders of the Rila Music Exchange project are Sofia Högstadius, a folk violinist from Sweden, and Myriam De Bonte, a diatonic accordion player from Belgium. Högstadius and De Bonte have both studied Bulgarian folk music traditions at the Plovdiv Academy of Music, Dance and Visual Art and have a great love for Bulgarian people and culture. The Rila project has provided a forum to spread this love, and knowledge about Bulgaria, to young musical enthusiasts from around Europe, as well as from as far away as Australia and Latin America.

The workshop is a total immersion in the music-making activity, based on the belief that music quickly fosters strong, meaningful, and lasting human relationships among the participants, regardless of their role. For me, the validity of this belief has been confirmed through my personal observation of the annual ethno music workshops held in Rila since 2012. Participants speak of the Rila Music Exchange as a life-changing experience—an opportunity to discover, as one participant put it, "the Rila ME."

If any one feature distinguishes the Rila Music Exchange from other music workshops of the Ethno type, it is the way the workshop incorporates collaborative music-making with local amateur musicians. This is not just a meeting of different cultures. It is a meeting of different *generations*, as the young foreign musicians are brought into close contact with residents of local villages, often twice or three times their age, for whom the performance of folk music is both a pastime and a way of preserving often-threatened local cultural traditions. Perhaps the most moving part of the Rila Music Exchange experience is to see how moved these aging Bulgarians are to realize just how important their music-making is to the young people who have traveled to Bulgaria to learn from and perform with them.

As with *In C* and Cobra Junior, the Rila Music Exchange project explores the ways that music is the ground and medium for human interaction among people who might otherwise assume that they had little in common, even if they all happen to sing or play musical instruments. Aside from any mutual desire to engage in this type of interaction, the mutual ability to communicate through entrainment-enabled music-making. Entrainment ensures that we are able to transcend other cultural barriers, allowing us to realize the potential of music-making to understanding and agreeing with each other—even if that agreement is not expressed in terms of traditional spoken or written language.

Bibliography

Adorno, Teodor W. Beethoven: The Philosophy of Music. Palo Alto, CA: Stanford University Press, 2002.

Alperson, Philip. "Introduction: The Philosophy of Music." In *What is Music? An Introduction to the Philosophy of Music*, edited by Philip Alperson. University Park: The Pennsylvania State University Press, 1987.

Barzun, Jacques. "Berlioz as man and thinker." In *The Cambridge Companion to Berlioz,* edited by Peter Bloom, 11-19. Cambridge: Cambridge University Press, 2000.

Bashford, Christina. "The String Quartet and Society." In *The Cambridge Companion to the String Quartet*, edited by Robin Stowell, 3–18. Cambridge: Cambridge University Press, 2003.

Batson, C. Daniel. "Empathy-Induced Altruistic Motivation." Chapter for Inaugural Herzliya Symposium on Prosocial Motives, Emotions, and Behavior, March 24–27, 2008. http://portal.idc.ac.il/en/symposium/herzliyasymposium/documents/dcbatson.pdf (last accessed on January 24, 2015).

Batson, C. Daniel. "Empathic Concern and Altruism in Humans." Online publication of *On the Human*, National Humanities Center, 2009. http://onthehuman.org/2009/10/empathic-concern-and-altruism-in-humans/ (last accessed on June 1, 2013).

Benjamin, Walter. "The Work of Art in the Age of Its Technological Reproducibility: Second Version." In *The Work of Art in the Age of Its Technological Reproducibility and Other Writings on Media*, edited by Michael William Jennings, Brigid Doherty, Thomas Y. Levin, and Edmund Jephcott, 19–55. Cambridge: Belnap Press, 2008.

Berlioz, Hector. "Euphonia, or the Musical City." In *Evenings with the Orchestra*, translated and edited by Jacques Barzun, 258–97. New York: Alfred A. Knopf, 1956.

Blanchot, Maurice. *The Gaze of Orpheus and Other Literary Essays*. Translated by Lydia Davis. Barrytown: Station Hill Press, 1981.

Bloom, Paul. "Feeling Sorry for Tsarnaev." *The New Yorker* online blog, May 16, 2013. http://www.newyorker.com/news/news-desk/feeling-sorry-for-tsarnaev (last accessed on January 22, 2015).

Bloom, Paul. "The Baby in the Well: The Case Against Empathy." *The New Yorker*, May 20, 2013.

Blum, David, and Guarneri Quartet. *The Art of Quartet Playing: The Guarneri Quartet in Conversation with David Blum*. Ithaca: Cornell University Press, 1986.

Boucher, Geoff. "The Politics of Aesthetic Affect: A Reconstruction of Habermas' Art Theory." *Parrhesia*, no. 13 (2011): 62–78.

Brogan, Walter A. *Heidegger and Aristotle: The Twofoldness of Being*. Albany: State University of New York Press, 2005.

Bujic, Bojan. "Notation and Realization: Musical Performance in Historical Perspective." In *The Interpretation of Music: Philosophical Essays*, edited by Michael Krausz. Oxford: Clarendon, 1995.

Busoni, Ferruccio. *Sketch of a New Esthetic of Music*. Translated by Theodore Baker. New York: G. Schirmer, 1911.

Cage, John. *Silence: Lectures and Writings*. Middletown: Wesleyan University Press, 1973.

Carter, Joseph P. "Heidegger's Sein zum Tode as radicalization of Aristotle's definition of kinesis." *Epoché: A Journal for the History of Philosophy* 18 (2) (Spring 2014): 473–502.

Clarke, Emma C. *Iamblichus' De mysteriis: A Manifesto of the Miraculous*. Aldershot: Ashgate, 2001.

Cross, Ian. "Music and Social Being." *Musicology Australia*, Vol. 28, no. 1 (2005): 114–126.

Cross, Ian. "Music as a social and cognitive process." In *Language and Music as Cognitive Systems,* edited by Patrick Rebuschat, Martin Rohrmeier, John A. Hawkins, and Ian Cross. London: Oxford University Press, 2011.

Cross, Ian. "Music, speech and meaning in interaction." Keynote address, 12th International Congress on Musical Signification, Louvain-la-Neuve, Belgium. April 2, 2013.

Czobor-Lupp, Mihaela. "Communicative Reason and Intercultural Understanding: A Critical Discussion of Habermas." *European Journal of Political Theory*, 7 (2008): 430–48.

Dalai Lama and Ekman, Paul. *Emotional Awareness: Overcoming the Obstacles to Psychological Balance and Compassion.* New York: Macmillan, 2008.

Danto, Arthur C. *Transfiguration of the Commonplace: A Philosophy of Art.* Cambridge: Harvard University Press, 1981.

Dean, Geoffrey. "Орфееви отражения в късните солови творби на Лазар Николов" в „Димитър Ненов и Лазар Николов—Аспекти на модерността в българска музика". Пловдив: АМТИИ, 2012 ("Orphic Reflections in the Late Solo Compositions of Lazar Nikolov." In *Aspects of Modernity in Bulgarian Music*, edited by Yulian Kuyumdzhiev. Plovdiv: Academy of Music, Dance, and Visual Art, 2012).

Dewey, John. *Art as Experience.* New York: Perigee, 1934.

Decety, Jean and Jackson, Philip L. "The Functional Architecture of Human Empathy." *Behavioral and Cognitive Neuroscience Reviews*, Vol. 3, no. 2, (2004): 71–100.

Descartes, Rene. *Discourse on the Method of Rightly Conducting One's Reason, and of Seeking Truth in the Sciences.* Translated by John Veitch. (Dent, 1912).

Dogantan-Dack, Mine. "'Phrasing—the Very Life of Music': Performing the Music and Nineteenth-Century Performance Theory." *Nineteenth-Century Music Review*, 9 (2012): 7–30.

Donath, Judith. "Signals, cues and meaning." In unpublished book manuscript, 2007. http://vivatropolis.com/judith/signalsTruthDesign.html (last accessed on January 24, 2015).

Drabkin, William. *A Reader's Guide to Haydn's Early Quartets.* Westport: Greenwood Publishing Group, 2000.

Dreyfus, Hubert L. "Heidegger on Art." Berkeley: University of California, 2008. http://sophos.berkeley.edu/dreyfus/ (last accessed on January 24, 2015).

Dubinsky, Rostislav. *Stormy Applause: Making Music in a Worker's State.* New York: Hill and Wang, 1989.

Duranti, Alessandro. "Husserl, intersubjectivity and anthropology." *Anthropological Theory*, Vol. 10, no. 1 (2010): 16–35.

Duvenage, Pieter. *Habermas and Aesthetics: The Limits of Communicative Reason.* Hoboken: Wiley, 2003.

Ekman, Paul. "The Roots of Empathy and Compassion." Lecture given at Greater Good Science Center of the University of California at Berkeley, 2010. http://youtu.be/3AgvKJK-nrk (last accessed on January 24, 2015).

Ekman, Paul. "Paul Ekman talks about Empathy with Edwin Rutsch." Interview for The Center for Building a Culture of Empathy, 2011. https://youtu.be/3i1QFv PtqM (last accessed on January 24, 2015).

Epstein, Jeffrey. Review of *The Politics of Care in Habermas and Derrida* (Ganis). *Plurilogue: Politics and Philosophy Reviews*, no. 11 (2012).

Feldman, Morton. *The Music of Morton Feldman.* Edited by Thomas DeLio. Oxford: Psychology Press, 1996.

Gadamer, Hans-Georg. *The Relevance of the Beautiful and Other Essays.* Edited by R. Bernasconi, translated by N. Walker. Cambridge: Cambridge University Press, 1986.

Gadamer, Hans-Georg. *Truth and Method.* Translated by Joel Weinsheimer and Donald G. Marshall. New York: Crossroad, 1992.

Gadamer, Hans-Georg. "The Universality of the Hermeneutical Problem." In *The Continental Philosophy Reader*, edited by Richard Kearney and Mara Rainwater, 111–21. New York: Routledge, 1995.

Gallagher, Shaun. "Empathy, simulation and narrative." *Science in Context*, Vol. 25, no. 3 (September 2012): 355–81.

Ganis, Richard. *The Politics of Care in Habermas and Derrida: Between Measurability and Immeasurability.* Lanham: Rowman and Littlefield, 2011.

Gilboa, Avi and Tal-Shmotkin, Malka. "String quartets as self-managed teams: An interdisciplinary perspective." *Psychology of Music*, Vol. 40, no. 1 (2012): 19–41.

Gilmore, John C. "Dewey and Gadamer on the Ontology of Art." *Man and World* 20, (1987): 205–19.

Glynn, Simon. "Identity, Intersubjectivity and Communicative Action." In *Proceedings of the Twentieth World Congress of Philosophy*. Boston: The Paideia Archive, 1998.

Grondin, Jean "Play, Festival and Ritual in Gadamer: On the theme of the immemorial in his later works." In *Language and Linguisticality in Gadamer's Hermeneutics,* translated by L. K. Schmidt, 43–50. Lanham: Lexington Books, 2001.

Habermas, Jürgen. *Moral Consciousness and Communicative Action.* Translated by C. Lenhardt and S. W. Nicolsen. Cambridge: MIT Press, 1990.

Habermas, Jürgen. *Justification and Application.* Translated by C. P. Cronin. Cambridge: MIT Press, 1993.

Habermas, Jürgen. "Communicative Ethics." In *The Inclusion of the Other: Studies in Political Theory*, edited by Ciaran P. Cronin and Pablo de Greiff. Cambridge: MIT Press, 1998.

Hegel, Georg Wilhelm Friedrich. *Hegel's Lectures on the History of Philosophy*. Translated by E. S. Haldane and F. H. Simpson. London: Routledge and Kegan Paul, 1892.

Heidegger, Martin. *Being and Time.* Translated by John Macquarrie and Edward Robinson. Oxford: Blackwell, 1962.

Heidegger, Martin. "The Origin of the Work of Art." In *Poetry, Language, Thought,* translated by Albert Hofstadter, 15–86. New York: Harper and Row, 1971.

Heidegger, Martin. *Basic Concepts of Ancient Philosophy*. Translated by Richard Rojcewicz. Bloomington: Indiana University Press, 2007.

Heidegger, Martin. *The Basic Problems of Phenomenology.* Translated by Albert Hofstadter. Bloomington: Indiana University Press, 1975.

Heidegger, Martin. *Becoming Heidegger: On the Trail of His Early Occasional Writings, 1910–1927.* Edited by Theodore Kisiel and Thomas Sheehan. Evanston: Northwestern University Press, 2007.

Heidegger, Martin. *Early Greek Thinking*. Translated by David F. Krell and Frank A. Capuzzi. New York, Harper and Row, 1975.

Heidegger, Martin. *The Event*. Translated by Richard Rojcewicz. Bloomington: Indiana University Press, 2013.

Heidegger, Martin. *Introduction to Metaphysics*. Translated by Gregory Fried and Richard Polt. New Haven: Yale University Press, 2000.

Heidegger, Martin. *Nietzsche I: The Will to Power as Art*. Translated by David F. Krell. New York, Harper and Row, 1979.

Heidegger, Martin. *Pathmarks*. Edited by William McNeill. Cambridge: Cambridge University Press, 1998.

Hindemith, Paul. *A Composer's World: Horizons and Limitations*. Mainz: Schott Musik International, 1952.

Horkheimer, Max and Adorno, Theodor W. *Dialectic of Enlightenment*. Translated by E. Jephcott. Palo Alto: Stanford University Press, 2002.

Huron, David. "Relish and Foreboding, Pain and Pleasure, Disappointment and Relief: The Role of Time in Hedonic Experience." Keynote address, 12th International Congress on Music Signification, Louvain-la-Neuve, Belgium, April 2, 2013.

Huron, David. "Understanding Music-Related Emotion: Lessons from Ethology." *Proceedings of the 12th International Conference on Music Perception and Cognition, Thessaloniki, Greece*. Edited by P. Cambouropoulos, C. Tsougras, P. Mavromatis, and K. Pastiadis. July 23–28, 2012. http://icmpcescom2012.web.auth.gr/sites/default/files/papers/473_Proc.pdf (last accessed on January 24, 2015).

Husserl, Edmund. *Cartesian Meditations*. Translated by Dorion Cairnes. The Hague: Nijhoff, 1970.

Ingram, David. *Reason, History, and Politics: The Communitarian Grounds of Legitimation in the Modern Age*. Albany: State University of New York Press, 1995.

Jung, Carl Gustav. *Visions: Notes of the Seminar Given in 1930–1934*, Vol. 1. Edited by Claire Douglas. Princeton: Princeton University Press, 1997.

Kearney, Richard. *Poetics of Imagining: Modern to Post-modern.* Edinburgh: Edinburgh University Press, 1998.

Kelly, Katherine. "The Orphic mouth in 'Not I'." In *The Beckett Studies Reader*, edited by S. E. Gontarski, 121–8. Gainesville: University Press of Florida, 1993.

Kevorkian, Margarita. „Животът ми е творчество". Интервю с Лазар Николов в Николов, Лазар: „Моят свят", 101–26. София: Лице, 1998 ("My Life is Creativity." Interview with Lazar Nikolov. In Nikolov, Lazar, *My World*, 101–26. Sofia: Litse, 1998).

Kockelmans, Joseph J. *Heidegger on Art and Art Works.* The Hague: Martinus Nijhoff, 1985.

Knight, Kelvin. "Aristotelianism versus Communitarianism." *Analyse & Kritik,* 27 (2005): 259–73.

Kohut, Heinz. "Reflections on Empathy." Speech given at Self Psychology conference in Berkeley, CA, 1981. https://youtu.be/ZQ6Y3hoKI8U (last accessed on January 24, 2015).

Kohut, Heinz. "Introspection, Empathy, and Psychoanalysis: An Examination of the Relationship Between Mode of Observation and Theory." *Journal of the American Psychoanalysis Association,* 7 (1959): 459–83.

Lee, M. Owen. *Virgil As Orpheus: A Study of the Georgics.* New York: SUNY Press, 1996.

Le Guin, Elisabeth. "'One Says that One Weeps, but One Does Not Weep: Sensible, Grotesque, and Mechanical Embodiments in Boccherini's Chamber Music." *Journal of the American Musicological Society* 55 (2002): 207–54.

Le Guin, Elisabeth. *Boccherini's Body: An Essay in Carnal Musicology.* Berkeley: University of California Press, 2005.

Lomax, Alan. "Song Structure and Social Structure." *Ethnology,* Vol. 1, no. 4 (1962): 425–51.

Lubans, Jr., John. "The Invisible Leader: Lessons for Leaders from the Orpheus Chamber Orchestra." *OD Practitioner*, Vol. 38, no. 2 (2006): 5–9.

MacIntyre, Alasdair. *After Virtue.* Notre Dame: University of Notre Dame Press, 1984.

Malaby, Thomas M. "Anthropology and play: the contours of playful experience." *New Literary History* 40/1 (2009): 205–18.

Malinowski, Bronisław. "The Problem of Meaning in Primitive Languages." In Supplement I to C. K. Ogden and I. A. Richards, *The Meaning of Meaning: A Study of the Influence of Language upon Thought and of the Science of Symbolism*, 296–336. Cambridge: University of Cambridge, 1923.

McGahey, Robert. *The Orphic Moment: Shaman to Poet-Thinker in Plato, Nietzsche, and Mallarme*. Albany: State University of New York Press, 1994.

McNeill, William. "Heidegger's Hölderlin Lectures" (2013). https://www.academia.edu/4407705/Heideggers_Holderlin_Lectures (last accessed on January 24, 2015).

Mirka, Agawu. *Communication in Eighteenth-Century Music*. Cambridge: Cambridge University Press, 2012.

Morrell, Michael E. *Empathy and Democracy: Feeling, Thinking, and Deliberation*. University Park: Pennsylvania State University Press, 2010.

Murnighan, J. Keith, and Conlon, Donald E. "The Dynamics of Intense Work Groups: A Study of British String Quartets." *Administrative Science Quarterly*, Vol. 36, no. 2 (1991): 165–86.

Nettl, Paul. *Mozart and Masonry*. New York: Philosophical Library, 1957.

Nikolov, Lazar. Анотация за неговата „Пиеса за маримба—Из музиката на Орфей I". София: Седмицата на американската музика в България, 2000 (Program note for *Piece for Marimba: From the Music of Orpheus I*. Sofia: American Music Week in Bulgaria, 2000).

Nikolov, Lazar. Мнение на Лазар Николов за преработката на Джефри Дийн на пиесата ми за виола соло за виолончело соло. Ръкопис, 2002 (Opinion of Lazar Nikolov concerning Geoffrey Dean's arrangement of my solo viola piece for cello solo. Sofia: Handwritten manuscript, 2002).

Nikolov, Lazar. Letter to Dimiter Christoff dated January 28. Sofia: Handwritten manuscript, 2003.

Nowell-Smith, David. "The Art of Fugue: Heidegger on Rhythm." *Gatherings: The Heidegger Circle Annual*, 2 (2012): 41–64.

Olivier, Bert. *Philosophy and the Arts: Collected Essays*. Bern: Peter Lang, 2009.

O'Dea, Jane. *Virtue or Virtuosity? Explorations in the Ethics of Musical Performance*. Westport and London: Greenwood Press, 2000.

Ovid. *Metamorphoses*. Translated by A. D. Melville. London: Oxford University Press, 2009.

Palmer, Richard E. *Hermeneutics: Interpretation Theory in Schleiermacher, Dilthey, Heidegger, and Gadamer*. Evanston: Northwestern University Press, 1969.

Palmer, Richard E. "Hermeneutics and the Disciplines: The Relevance of Gadamer's Philosophical Hermeneutics to Thirty-Six Topics or Fields of Human Activity." Lecture delivered at Southern Illinois University, Carbondale, 1999. http://www.mac.edu/faculty/richardpalmer/relevance.html (last accessed on January 24, 2015).

Petrova, Angelina. „Композиторът Лазар Николов". София: Институт по изкуствознание при БАН, 2003 (*The Composer Lazar Nikolov*. Sofia: Bulgarian Academy of Sciences, 2003).

Plato. "Theaetetus." In *The Dialogues of Plato,* translated by Benjamin Jowett, Vol. 4, 193–280 (Oxford: Clarendon Press, 1892).

Rameson, Lian T. and Lieberman, Matthew D. "Empathy: A Social Cognitive Neuroscience Approach." *Social and Personality Psychology Compass* 3/1 (2009): 94–110.

Reich, Steve. *Writings on Music: 1965–2000*. Edited by Paul Hillier. Oxford: Oxford University Press, 2002.

Reichardt, Johann Friedrich. From *Briefe geschrieben auf einer Reise nach Wien*. In *Source Readings in Music History: The Classic Era*, selected and annotated by Oliver Strunk, 154–66. New York: Norton, 1965.

Ricoeur, Paul. *Hermeneutics and the Human Sciences*. Translated by J. B. Thompson. Cambridge: University of Cambridge Press, 1981.

Ricoeur, Paul. "Imagination in discourse and action." In *Rethinking Imagination: Culture and Creativity*, edited by Gillian Robinson and John F. Rundell, 118–35. London: Routledge, 1994.

Rilke, Rainer Maria. *Ahead of All Parting: The Selected Poetry and Prose of Rainer Maria Rilke.* Edited and translated by Stephen Mitchell. New York: The Modern Library, 1995.

Rorty, Richard. *Consequences of Pragmatism.* Minneapolis: University of Minnesota Press, 1982.

Rowell, Louis. *Thinking About Music.* Amherst: University of Massachusetts Press, 1985.

Rumph, Stephen. *Mozart and Enlightenment Semiotics.* Berkeley: University of California Press, 2011.

Schafer, R. Murray. *The Soundscape: Our Sonic Environment and the Tuning of the World.* Rochester: Destiny Books, 1977.

Sewell, Elizabeth. *The Orphic Voice: Poetry and Natural History.* New Haven: Yale University Press, 1960.

Sheehan, Thomas. "Being, Opened-ness, and Unlimited Technology: Ten Theses on Heidegger." *PortiQue: Revue de philosophie et de sciences humaines,* 18 (2006): 1253–9.

Sheehan, Thomas. "The Turn." In *Heidegger: Key Concepts,* edited by Bret W. Davis, 82–101. Durham: Acumen Publishing, 2009.

Sheehan, Thomas. "Facticity and Ereignis." In *Interpreting Heidegger: New Essays,* edited by Daniel Dahlstrom, 42–68. Cambridge: Cambridge University Press, 2011.

Shusterman, Richard. "Pragmatism Between Aesthetic Experience and Aesthetic Education." *Studies in Philosophy and Education,* Vol. 22, no. 5 (2003): 403–12.

Small, Christopher. *Musicking: The Meanings of Performing and Listening.* Middletown: Wesleyan University Press, 1998.

Solomon, Maynard. *Mozart: A Life.* New York: HarperCollins, 2009.

Strauss, Walter A. *Descent and return: The Orphic Theme in Modern Literature.* Cambridge: Harvard University Press, 1971.

Taminiaux, Jacques. "On Heidegger's Interpretation of the Will to Power as Art." *New Nietzsche Studies,* Vol. 3, nos. 1 and 2 (1999): 1–22.

Tatarkiewicz, Władysław. "Art and Poetry: A Contribution to the History of Ancient Aesthetics." *Studia Logica Journal* of the Institute of Philosophy and Sociology of the Polish Academy of Sciences (ca. 1940): 367–418.

Toi, Miho, and C. Daniel Batson. "More Evidence That Empathy is a Source of Altruistic Motivation." *Journal of Personality and Social Psychology*, Vol. 43, no. 2 (August 1982): 281–92.

Ure, Michael. *Nietzsche's Therapy: Self-cultivation in the Middle Works*. Lanham: Lexington Books, 2008.

Uzdavinys, Algis. *Orpheus and the Roots of Platonism*. London: The Matheson Trust, 2011.

Valchinova-Chendova, Elizaveta. „Музиката на Димитър Христов като сугестивна въображаема многолинейност: пространство отструктурирани и разгърнати звукови архетупи". Българско музикознание 3–4 (2013): 201–26 ("The Music of Dimiter Christoff as a Suggestive Imaginary Multilinearity: Space of Structured and Developed Sound Archetypes." Bulgarian Musicology, 3–4 (2013): 201–226).

Vetlesen, Arne Johan. *Perception, Empathy, and Judgment: An Inquiry into the Preconditions of Moral Performance*. University Park: Pennsylvania State University Press, 1994.

West, David. *Continental Philosophy: An Introduction*. Hoboken: Wiley, 2010.

Wittgenstein, Ludwig. *Philosophical Investigations*. Translated by Gertrude Elizabeth Margaret Anscombe. New York: Macmillan, 1958.

Wittgenstein, Ludwig. *Tractatus Logico-Philosophicus*. Translated by David Francis Pears and Brian McGuinness. New York: Routledge, 1961.

Wolterstorff, Nicholas. "The Work of Making a Work of Music." In *What Is Music? An Introduction to the Philosophy of Music*, edited by Philip Alperson, 101–30. University Park: Pennsylvania State University Press, 1987.

Young, Julian. *Heidegger's Philosophy of Art*. Cambridge: Cambridge University Press, 2001.

Zupancic, Metka. "In the Beginning Was the Word: Reflections on Gerard Bucher's *L'imagination de l'origine*." In *In Death, Language, Thought: On Gérard Bucher's L'imagination de l'origine*, 51–58. Birmingham: Summa Publications, 2005.

Zahavi, Dan. "Simulation, Projection and Empathy." *Consciousness and Cognition* 17 (2008): 514–22.

Index

A

Adams, John, 36
Adorno, Theodor W., 45, 70–71, 139, 144
aesthetic experience, 46, 48, 49
    active participation, 52, 97, 98–103, 117
    continuity of, 39, 47
    emotion in, 46, 49, 50
    increase in being, 23, 51
    perception in, 8, 47, 49–51, 54, 60, 65, 80, 81, 87, 88, 89, 90, 94, 121, 124, 128, 132
    phases of, 46, 49
aesthetics, 7, 8, 13–14, 18–19, 39–42, 44–56, 80, 98, 100, 103, 120–21, 127–28
aleatory, 34
aletheia, 7, 14, 17–23, 25, 29, 31–33, 51
allegory, 59, 68
analytical philosophy, 9, 42, 81
Apollo, 62–65, 70
Ardenza Foundation, 9, 133, 137
Aristotle, 15–16, 18, 24, 30–31, 41, 43, 44, 59, 61, 140
art
    as community of experience, 44–51, 53, 56
    as happening of truth, 34
    as something past, 18, 28
    as task for thinking, 54
    Erlebniskunst, 46
    worlds initiated by, 26, 31

B

Bach, Carl Philipp Emanuel, 90, 93
Bach, Johann Sebastian, 70
beauty, 32–33, 44
    unity with truth, 18
Beckett, Samuel, 69, 145
Beethoven, Ludwig van, 70–71, 109, 139
Benjamin, Walter, 13, 45
Berlioz, Hector, 102–4, 139
Bespalov, Nikolai, 114
Blanchot, Maurice, 59, 66, 68–69, 140
Boccherini, Luigi, 92, 145
Bucher, Gérard, 60, 150
Bulgarian concert venues
    Boris Christoff Center, 133
    Bulgaria Hall, 116
    Bulgarian National Radio, 134, 135
    National Palace of Culture, 116
Bulgarian educational institutions
    American University in Bulgaria, 9
    Bourgas National Music School, 134
    National Music Academy, 134
    Plovdiv Academy of Music, Dance and Visual Art, 137
    Sofia University, 9
Bulgarian music ensembles
    Ardenza Trio, 134
    Dimov Quartet, 9, 114–16
    Gabrovo Chamber Orchestra, 92
    Plovdiv Philharmonic Orchestra, 72
    Sofia Philharmonic Orchestra, 114
    Sofia Quartet, 9, 114, 116–18
    Stankov-Radionov Duo, 9
Bulgarian music festivals
    AmBul, 133

American Music Week in
Bulgaria, 72, 133, 146
Musica Nova, 92
Rila Music Exchange, 9, 136–38
Busoni, Ferruccio, 70–71, 140

C

Cage, John, 34, 35, 140
chamber music, 8, 9, 92, 97, 106–18
Chaplin, Charles, 37
Christoff, Dimiter, 8, 9, 73, 78, 92–94, 146, 149
  Reflections of a Lonely Violoncello, 92
Cocteau, Jean, 67
communitarianism, 8, 97–118, 136, 144
compassion, 79, 85, 125
consensual empathic manipulation, 8, 77, 78, 89, 93, 94
creative Orphic intersubjectivity, 7, 59, 73–75
creative process, 7, 8, 35, 46, 50, 56, 59, 61–63, 65, 67–75, 92, 93, 101, 133–38
Cross, Ian, 77, 119, 129–30, 140, 141

D

Dalai Lama, 85, 141
Dalley, John, 113
De Bonte, Myriam, 9, 137
Descartes, René, 20, 74, 81, 141, 144
Dewey, John, 7, 8, 13, 39–56, 90, 98, 141, 143
  Art as Experience, 13, 39–42, 44–56, 90, 141
Diderot, Denis, 108
Dimitrov, Georgi, 72
Dimov, Dimo, 114–16, 118
Dionysos, 62–65, 70

Dreyfus, Hubert L., 23, 33–34, 141
Dubinsky, Rostislav, 112, 113, 115, 142

E

Einstein, Albert, 36
Ekman, Paul, 85–86, 141, 142
empathy, 8, 9, 73–75, 77–86, 94, 124, 122–27
  affective component, 79, 82, 85, 86, 89, 91–92, 124–25
  biological component, 80
  caring component, 83–86, 123–27
  cognitive component, 79, 84–85, 123–27, 132
  Einfühlung, 74, 79, 80
  empatheia, 79
  empathic response, 78, 79, 83–86, 89–94, 126
  imaginative transfer, 7, 8, 74–75, 79, 93
  mindreading, 82
  motor mimicry, 81, 82
  simulation theory, 81–83, 86
Enlightenment (Age of), 34, 44, 70, 92, 93, 106–10, 144, 146, 148
entrainment, 8, 119, 130, 132, 138
ethics, 8, 18, 69, 77, 90, 95, 119–22, 123–25, 130, 131, 126–33, 134, 140, 143, 147
ethology, 41, 78, 86, 87, 88
evolutionary naturalism, 40, 42, 53
existentialism, 16, 24, 25, 28, 41–42, 66, 74

F

facticity, 20, 21, 24, 27–28, 32, 55
Feldman, Morton, 35, 142
freemasonry, 108

G

Gadamer, Hans-Georg, 7, 8, 14, 35, 39–41, 44–56, 70, 97–98, 100–101, 101, 123, 142, 143, 147
  alienation of aesthetic consciousness, 14
  festival (theory of), 9, 53, 55, 97, 100–101
  fusion of horizons, 53, 101
  play (theory of), 46, 48–49, 50, 52, 54, 55, 97, 100–101, 146
  The Relevance of the Beautiful, 35, 44–56, 101, 142
  Truth and Method, 39, 46, 48, 142
Gandhi, Mahatma, 36
Geier, Laura, 9
Gerov, Valentin, 72, 73
Glass, Philip, 36–38
Goethe, Johann Wolfgang von, 107
Greek architecture, 23, 26, 29, 30, 32, 54
Greek mythology, 7, 19, 59–69
Greek-to-Latin translation, 17, 33

H

Habermas, Jürgen, 8, 40, 39–44, 119–33, 140, 141, 142, 143
  aesthetics, 119–33, 127–28, 131
  communicative action, 121–23, 131–33
  discourse ethics, 119–23, 126–28, 132–33, 136
  mutual perspective taking, 9, 122–27
  practical discourse, 119–23, 127, 132–33
  unity of reason, 44, 119–23
Haydn, Joseph, 107, 106–10, 141
Hegel, Georg Wilhelm Friedrich, 13–23, 25–27, 30–33, 35, 41, 42–44, 53, 70, 73, 120, 143
  and universal Truth, 15, 20, 21–23
  dialectic, 15, 20, 25, 31
  Lectures on the History of Philosophy, 13, 15, 17, 19, 20, 22, 26, 27, 30
Heidegger, Martin, 7, 24–29, 13–38, 39–40, 42–43, 51, 60–62, 81, 98, 143–44
  Being and Time, 13–31, 33, 143
  Dasein, 13–18, 19–23, 23, 24–29, 30, 32, 33
  hermeneutic circle, 16, 41
  illuminating projection, 14, 23–33, 60
  motion, 17, 27–31
  onthological Interpretation, 15, 18, 21, 25, 28, 31, 140, 147, 148
  The Open, 14, 25–27
  The Origin of the Work of Art, 13–18, 23, 25–34, 60, 62, 143
hermeneutics, 7, 16, 35, 39–43, 46, 50, 51–52, 55, 60, 64, 74, 75, 98, 120, 123
Hermes, 62, 65, 69–70, 75
Hindemith, Paul, 104, 110, 144
historicity, 24, 27–31
history of philosophy, 13–23, 27, 30, 31–33, 35, 40–44, 120, 143
Högstadius, Sophia, 9, 137
Holocaust, 36
Homer, 63, 64
Huron, David, 77, 78, 86–90, 144
Husserl, Edmund, 7, 14, 59, 73–75, 79, 142, 144

I

I-Ching, 34
identification (cognitive act), 7, 8, 49, 50, 67, 73–75, 78, 79, 90–94, 102, 104, 124–26
Illuminati, Order of the, 108

imagination, 63–64
imagination (theories of), 7–9, 40–41, 46, 50, 56, 59–61, 62, 65–75, 79, 93, 98, 124, 125, 128, 135, 150
improvisation, 8, 35, 36, 52, 71–75, 133–38
inspiration, 7, 9, 35, 59–61, 61–62, 65, 67, 68–69
intentionality, 119, 129
intercultural relations, 7–9, 116–18, 128, 133, 136–38
interpretation, 7–9, 20, 21, 25, 27, 31, 35, 37, 46, 50, 52, 54, 59, 60, 62, 64–70, 71, 72, 73–75, 92–94, 104–18, 131, 133–36, 138
interpretative Orphic intersubjectivity, 8, 78, 92–94
intersubjectivity, 7–9, 14, 21–26, 27–31, 42, 53, 56, 59, 73–75, 78, 79, 93, 121, 122–23, 127, 129–33, 142
irreducibility, 14, 55
Ives, Charles, 34

J

James, William, 39
jazz, 35, 36, 135
Jeunesses Musicales, 136
Jung, Carl, 59, 68–69, 144

K

Kafka, Franz, 69
Kant, Immanuel, 14, 41–46, 50, 60, 73, 92, 120, 121, 124
Keats, John, 40, 41
Kleiber, Carlos, 104
Kohlberg, Lawrence, 122, 124
Kohut, Heinz, 79, 81, 84–85, 145
Koleva, Tatiana, 72
Korot, Beryl, 36
Koyaanisqatsi, 36–38

Kozev, Dimiter, 115

L

language, 23, 31–33, 42–44, 51, 55, 59, 60–61, 69, 78, 80, 107, 128–29, 130, 138
Le Guin, Elisabeth, 91–92, 145
liberalism, 8, 106–14, 118
lifeworld, 14, 42, 44, 120, 127–28, 131
Lipps, Theodor, 80–81
Liszt, Franz, 90
Lomax, Alan, 77, 145

M

MacIntyre, Alasdair, 8, 98–99, 100, 145
Marcuse, Herbert, 66
Mead, John Gilbert, 122
metaphor, 59–61, 63–69, 73–75, 101, 107, 128
Mingus, Charles, 35, 36
minimalism, 35, 36–38, 133, 147
Mozart, Leopold, 107
Mozart, Wolfgang Amadeus, 70, 106–10, 146, 148
multimodality, 8, 77, 86–91
muses, 61, 62
musical collaboration, 7–9, 59, 71–75, 78, 92–94, 97, 106–18, 120, 127–33, 133–38
musical notation, 70, 71, 93, 140
musicking, 97, 98–103, 117, 148
music-making, 7, 8, 98–103, 105, 107–10, 112, 117, 119–20, 127–33, 137, 138

N

Nedelcheva, Ganka, 92
Nenov, Dimiter, 71
neoplatonic philosophy, 62, 140

Nietzsche, Friedrich, 13, 18, 42, 64, 66, 144, 146, 148, 149
Nikolov, Lazar, 7, 9, 59, 69, 71–75, 92, 141, 145, 146, 147
From the Music of Orpheus, 7, 59, 71–75, 146

O

Obama, Barack, 125
ontology, 15, 22, 25, 27–31, 33, 40, 45, 69, 74, 143
Orpheus, 7, 59–75, 77, 90, 92, 140, 141, 145, 146, 148, 149
  and Eurydice, 8, 65, 67, 68–69, 73, 75
  myth interpretations, 7, 59, 64–70
Orpheus Chamber Orchestra, 105–6, 145
Ovid, 66, 147
Ovsepyan, Petros, 8, 78, 93

P

Partch, Harry, 34
Peirce, Charles S., 78, 86
performance, 7, 8, 35, 46, 50, 52, 62, 64, 69, 73, 89, 90–94, 97, 99–101, 103, 104–18, 133–38
phenomenology, 7, 14, 15, 59, 73–75, 79, 81, 142, 144
Philosophy (critique of), 20, 21, 39–44, 148
Plato, 23, 41, 44, 59, 61–62, 146, 147
poet-musician, 59–75, 140, 145, 149
poetry, 23, 31, 59, 60–64, 68, 107
  as projective saying, 14, 23, 31, 60, 63, 67
postmodernism, 121
pragmatism, 7, 8, 13, 43, 39–56, 90, 98, 120, 141, 143, 148
Prokofiev, Sergei, 34

R

Ravnopolska, Anna-Maria, 92
Rawls, John, 122
Reggio, Godfrey, 36–38
Reich, Steve, 35, 36, 147
Reichardt, Johann Friedrich, 108–11, 147
Ricoeur, Paul, 7, 59–60, 60, 64–65, 67, 73–75, 147
  semantic innovation, 7, 60, 64, 73
Riley, Terry, 133, 138
Rilke, Rainer Maria, 59, 67, 68, 148
Romanticism, 34, 63, 65, 71, 102, 104
Rorty, Richard, 39–44, 148
Rousseau, Jean-Jacques, 108

S

Sartre, John-Paul, 41, 66
Scheler, Max, 81, 86
Schiller, Friedrich, 100
Schoenberg, Arnold, 34
Schupannzigh, Ignaz, 109
scientific method, 40
self-determination, 101
Selman, Robert L., 123
Shakespeare, William, 41
Sheehan, Thomas, 23, 24, 26, 30, 143, 148
Shelley, Percy Bysshe, 70
Shirokoliyska, Maria, 72
signals and cues, 49, 78, 86–89, 90, 94, 135, 136, 141
Small, Christopher, 97, 99–101, 117, 148
Smith, Adam, 81
Soyer, David, 113
Stoyanov, Ivan, 92
Stravinsky, Igor, 34, 90
string quartet, 8, 97, 106–18
  American style, 109–14, 116–18

as social unit, 111–12
control model, 97, 109–14, 114–16
conversation model, 97, 109–14, 116–18, 140
ensembles, 9, 106–18, 140
European style, 109–14, 114–16

T

Talgam, Itay, 104–5
techne, 35
technology, 37, 102, 120
temporality, 16, 17, 25, 27–31, 39, 53, 119, 130, 132
tradition, 8, 16, 27, 31, 34, 43, 39–44, 44, 51, 53, 75, 77, 91, 98–101, 114, 118, 120, 131, 137, 138
transcription, 71
Tree, Michael, 116

U

utilitarianism, 40
utopia, 97, 102

V

Van Gogh, Vincent, 32
Vladigerov, Pancho, 71

W

Wagner, Richard, 23
Weishaupt, Adam, 108
work of art, 15–18, 23–33, 34, 35, 37, 45, 46, 47, 50, 51–56, 60, 98
as collaborative process, 7, 8, 59, 68, 101, 135
as commody, 45
as something to perform, 7, 98
as thrust in history, 35
deobjectification of, 98
essence of, 17, 20, 44, 48, 53, 68
hermeneutic identity of, 35, 46, 52, 98
ontological functions of, 33

Y

Yordanov, Zdravko, 92
Yossifov, Dragomir, 9, 72

Z

Zen Buddhism, 34
Zorn, John, 135–36